Table of Contents

From Rule to Reality

Benedictine Practices Then and Now

by

Dr. ant

From Rule to Reality: Benedictine Practices Then and Now

Contents

Introduction

The tales of Saints Benedict and Scholastica are not mere historical anecdotes confined to the annals of medieval chronicles. Instead, they represent monumental pillars that hold up the edifice of Christian monasticism and spiritual discipline. Their lives, intrinsically intertwined yet diverse, reveal a profound spirituality that transcends epochs and geographical boundaries. Their influence has pervaded both the physical realm—through the establishment of monasteries and communities—and the metaphysical, in the realm of thought and devotional life.

We find ourselves in a world disjointed, searching for meaning in the ephemeral. The timeless teachings of Benedict and Scholastica offer a sanctuary of constancy, where one can retreat and rejuvenate the soul. Through their principles, they provide a moral compass, a blueprint guiding one towards a notion of an ideal society, while also preparing each individual for the trials and tumult of earthly existence.

In contemplating the lives of these saintly siblings, we must engage with the allegorical richness and philosophical underpinnings of their journey. Born into a society where the vestiges of the Roman Empire were crumbling, both Benedict and Scholastica responded not with despondency but with the ardor of spiritual reformers. They envisaged a utopian existence within the confines of monastic walls, aiming not just for personal salvation, but for the redemption of a fragmented society.

Their narrative begins in the heart of Italy, amidst a landscape both verdant and tumultuous. This environment, symbolic of the human condition, becomes the backdrop against which personal histories and divine interventions unfold. Benedict's journey from Rome to Subiaco, and ultimately to Monte Cassino, is marked by significant trials and divine revelations. Scholastica, often seen as an ethereal counterpart to her more documented brother, complements this journey with her own profound spirituality.

Though the temporal realm has witnessed the rise and fall of innumerable civilizations, the Rule of Saint Benedict remains steadfast. Crafted with a precision that balances discipline and compassion, the Rule is not merely a code of monastic life; it is an intricate tapestry of spiritual philosophy. It informs and shapes the daily rhythms of those who have chosen the contemplative path. Within its precepts, one can discern the fine line between human frailty and divine aspiration.

Scholastica, too, contributed significantly, her role serving to dispel the misconception that early Christian monasticism was an exclusively male domain. Her interactions with Benedict, steeped in both sibling affection and spiritual mentorship, underscore the importance of gender balance in spiritual endeavors. Her life exemplifies that sanctity is not confined by gender; it is universally accessible, provided one seeks it with genuine devotion.

In the celestial dance between work and prayer, Benedict and Scholastica choreographed a life that celebrated both action and contemplation. This delicate equilibrium is essential for anyone aspiring to lead a meaningful existence. By engaging in community labor, be it agricultural or scholarly, one finds expression and fulfillment. Meanwhile, prayer and contemplative practices anchor the soul, imbuing daily activities with divine grace.

Education also finds a venerable place within Benedictine tradition. The illuminated manuscripts painstakingly copied in the monasteries are not just relics of the past but are beacons of knowledge that ignited the intellectual revival of the Western world. Benedictines have long been custodians of wisdom, bridging the chasm between antiquity and the Renaissance. The fruits of their labor still echo in modern institutions of learning, preserving the continuity of thought and faith.

The influence of Benedict and Scholastica is not a stagnant legacy; it is dynamic, influencing various spheres from ecclesiastical art to social teachings. Their principles permeate the modern-day advocacy for social justice, providing a theological foundation that insists on the dignity and worth of every individual. The Cluniac reforms, for instance, stand as testament to the enduring and adaptive nature of Benedictine thought.

To view Benedict and Scholastica merely as historical figures is to miss the essence of their contribution. Their lives are a tapestry woven with strands of profound humility, incredible foresight, and divine inspiration. They beckon us to delve into a deeper understanding of their legacies, encouraging us to mold our lives through practices of prayer, work, and community engagement.

The text that follows will journey through the myriad aspects of Benedictine life, examining each element with the rigor of a historian and the contemplative gaze of a theologian. It will explore not just the inception of Benedictine monasticism but its evolution, mutations, and enduring relevance. Each chapter aims to unfold a layer, revealing how the lives and teachings of these saints continue to guide and inspire.

As we traverse through this exploration, the wisdom of Benedict and Scholastica will serve as both compass and lantern, illuminating our path and pointing us toward higher ideals. Their integrated approach to spirituality and everyday life holds lessons invaluable for contemporary seekers. In the immortal words of scriptures, their teachings are like "a lamp to the feet and a light to the path," inviting us to partake in a journey of transformation and enlightenment.

Thus, embark on this exploration not merely as a historical inquiry but as a spiritual pilgrimage. Allow the wisdom of Saints Benedict and Scholastica to permeate your consciousness, guiding you to a more profound comprehension of life's profound mysteries. Through their lives, we glimpse the contours of an existence that marries the temporal with the eternal, the mundane with the divine.

Chapter 1: Origins of Benedictine Monasticism

The seeds of Benedictine monasticism took root in the midst of a world yearning for spiritual and communal rejuvenation. Emerging from the spiritual fervor of the early Christian communities, this movement found its initial form in the confluence of scriptural devotion and communal living. As the early Christians grappled with the challenge of embodying their faith in a fractious society, it was Saint Benedict of Nursia whose vision crystallized these aspirations into a coherent monastic tradition. Inspired by earlier contemplative practices and communal endeavors, Benedict devised a rule that balanced prayer, work, and study, setting the foundation for a way of life that transcended mere religious observance. His twin sister, Saint Scholastica, further enriched this burgeoning tradition, embodying an equal fervency for spiritual discipline within her own community. Together, they not only articulated an ideal of contemplative life but also crafted a resilient framework that would withstand the vicissitudes of centuries, shaping both the spiritual and cultural landscape of Western Christianity.

Development of Early Christian Communities

The development of early Christian communities was a beacon of spiritual fervor and communal cohesion, setting the stage for what would eventually sculpt the Benedictine monastic tradition. These nascent gatherings of the faithful were marked by a shared devotion that transcended the chaos of the declining Roman Empire. Embodying an almost utopian yearning for divine connection, these communities became sanctuaries of hope, seeding the ideals of piety, humility, and communal living. Through their shared labor and collective prayer, they forged bonds that mirrored the early philosophical notions of an ideal society. This symbiotic blend of faith and fellowship laid the groundwork for later monastic endeavors, where Saints Benedict and Scholastica would find fertile ground for their divine calling. Thus, the early Christian communities did more than survive; they thrived as living allegories of the heavenly kingdom, echoing the uncomplicated but profound truths that would later resonate through Benedict's Rule.

Influence of Saint Augustine's Rule captures a pivotal moment in the development of early Christian monasticism, a deeply transformative era that reverberates through the corridors of history to this very day. Saint Augustine's rule stands as a precursor to the renowned Rule of Saint Benedict, establishing tenets that emphasize community, discipline, and the pursuit of spiritual goals. This sub-section illuminates how Augustine's vision and precepts laid foundational stones for what would become one of the most influential monastic rules in the Christian tradition.

Augustine of Hippo, a towering figure in early Christian theology, crafted a rule intending to create a life bound by unity and charity, reflecting the heavenly order on earth. This vision directly influenced the formation of monastic communities, shaping their inner dynamics and spiritual atmospheres. Augustine's Rule, known for its emphasis on communal living, pivoted around the concept of an 'ordered society' where each member contributes to the common good, avoiding excess and embracing temperance. Central to this rule was the notion that material possessions were communal, echoing the early Christian community described in the Acts of the Apostles.

It is in this landscape that Saint Benedict found fertile ground for his own innovations. Benedict did not discard Augustine's principles but rather built upon them, weaving Augustine's focus on community and piety into a comprehensive guide for monastic life. Augustine's Rule, with its call for daily prayer, manual labor, and mutual love, provided a template that would inspire Benedict's more elaborate structuring of monastic rigor and devotion. This seamless continuity of spiritual thought underscores the natural evolution from Augustine to Benedict, one that would shape Western monasticism for centuries.

Benedict's Rule, encapsulating yet distinguishing itself from Augustine's, introduced an organizational genius that ensured the sustainability and expansion of monastic communities. Augustine's influence is discernible in Benedict's understanding of monasticism as a communal act of worship and mutual support. By emphasizing the collective over the individual, Augustine's rule harmonized with Benedict's ideals of stability, obedience, and conversion of life. The monastery, under Augustine's vision and Benedict's implementation, became a microcosm of the heavenly city, a foretaste of eternal communion with the divine.

However, Benedict's contributions extend Augustine's rule through a more precise framework and detailed regulations, addressing practical aspects of monastic life with refreshing pragmatism. This specificity is perhaps what allowed Benedictine monasticism to flourish across different cultures and epochs. Augustine's influence is not merely a historical footnote but an indispensable part of the broader narrative of Christian monasticism. Without Augustine's theological groundwork, Benedict's revolutionary expansion might not have had the same resounding impact.

In both rules, there is a palpable tension between the ideals of solitude and community, withdrawal and participation. Augustine's vision infused the collective dimension with a robust theological grounding, while Benedict's implementation leaned heavily on structure and clear regulations. Together, they created a balanced approach to monastic life, harmonizing the individual's spiritual ascent with the community's overall welfare. This balance fostered an environment where monks could cultivate personal holiness while contributing to a living institution of faith and service.

A critical aspect of Augustine's Rule that resonates through Benedict's teachings is the elevation of communal worship. The rhythm of liturgical hours, the pulse of Psalms, and the cycle of prayers formed the beating heart of the monastic community. Augustine's blueprint for an ordered life of prayer and work ('ora et labora') found an echo in Benedict's detailed timetables for daily activities. The integration of liturgical life as a form of communal identity became a lasting legacy of Augustine's influence on Benedictine monasticism.

Furthermore, the concept of leadership within the community bears Augustine's imprint. Augustine portrayed the superior not as an overlord but as a servant to the servants of God, a shepherd tending the flock. Benedict refined this with his concept of the "abbot," who, while charged with authority, was also fundamentally a spiritual father accountable for the souls in his care. This nuanced approach to leadership, rooted in humility and service, underscores Augustine's deep and abiding impact on Benedict's governance model.

The emphasis on internal regulation over external compulsion and the priority of love over law found in Augustine's thoughts were passed down to Benedict. Benedict valued voluntary commitment and internal transformation more than mere mechanical adherence to rules. This ethos is reflective of Augustine's belief that true adherence to monastic life sprang from a heart transformed by love and grace. Benedict's Rule, with its adaptability and mercy, often echoes Augustine's concern for the interior life and the cultivation of virtue over strict legalism.

The long arc of history demonstrates how Augustine's initial blueprint was not only preserved but also amplified by Benedict's organizational genius. The symbiosis of their teachings ensured that monastic life remained relevant and adaptable through the Middle Ages and into modern times. Their combined influence has left an indelible mark on Christian spirituality, threading through the lived experience of countless monastic communities over the centuries.

In summation, **Influence of Saint Augustine's Rule** on Benedictine monasticism is profound and multifaceted. Augustine's focus on community, prayer, and spiritual leadership provided essential elements that Benedict would later refine and codify into a more detailed and enduring rule. Together, their spiritual legacies forge a continuum of monastic wisdom that charts a path toward divine contemplation within the embrace of communal life. Their combined influence transcends historical and cultural boundaries, offering a timeless model of Christian living that continues to inspire today.

Chapter 2: Life of Saint Benedict

Saint Benedict, born in the region of Nursia around 480 AD, stands as a monumental figure whose life and actions would revolutionize monasticism and Christian thought forever. His early years, shaped by a profound sense of spiritual seeking, were marked by immersion in the scriptures and the Interwoven influences of early Christian teachings. Striving for a life that mirrored his inner ideals, Benedict retreated to the solitude of Subiaco, where he lived as a hermit, paving the way for his spiritual ascension. The founding of Monte Cassino emerged not as a quest for grandeur, but as a profound experiment in communal living guided by divine inspiration. Here, amidst the olive groves and stony hills, Benedict laid down the blueprint for what would become the Rule, a testament to equilibrium, discipline, and spiritual labor. Facing adversities and skepticisms, he molded a robust community that harmonized prayer, work, and contemplation, grounding the ethos that each soul is both a participant and beneficiary of divine grace. Whether in seasons of harvest or times of austerity, Saint Benedict's life encapsulates a journey of unwavering faith and unyielding perseverance, embedding a legacy that continues to illuminate the paths of countless monks and laypeople across the centuries.

Childhood and Early Years

Saint Benedict, born around 480 AD in Nursia, which is present-day Norcia, Italy, emerged from a milieu of Roman affluence and civic duty. The early demise of Rome cast a shadow of unrest, compelling his noble family to seek solace and stability. From this crucible of upheaval, young Benedict bore witness to both the fragility and tenacity of human existence. This duality imbued his formative years with a sense of divine purpose and temporal urgency. Engulfed in the philosophies of the time, Benedict's youth was a tapestry of scholastic endeavors and spiritual musings, foreshadowing the ascetic path he would eventually embrace. It was here, in these embryonic days, that the seeds of monastic discipline were sown, nurtured by an intrinsic quest for a utopian society bound by sacred principles.

Education and Early Influences nestled in the verdant valleys of Nursia, a tapestry of faith and nature enveloped young Benedict and Scholastica. Here, the seeds of piety and discipline sowed in their youthful hearts took root. As children, they were exposed to the teachings of well-versed mentors and nurtured by a family deeply devoted to Christian values. These early lessons, entwined with the beauty of creation around them, became the bedrock of their spiritual journeys.

Their homeland, amidst the Apennine Mountains, was not merely a backdrop but a formative enclave where the confluence of nature and divine instruction shaped their characters. In a land where the chirping of birds harmonized with the chanting of scriptures, their minds opened to the sublime mysteries of existence. The elders of Nursia, steeped in wisdom and grace, imparted to the siblings the virtues of humility, charity, and rigorous study.

In those formative years, the young Benedict exhibited an innate thirst for knowledge and spiritual depth. His intellectual pursuits were not just scholastic but a quest to understand the divine will and moral order. Benedict was guided through the classical education system of the time, with an instruction steeped in the liberal arts—grammar, rhetoric, and logic. Yet his deepest contemplations often wandered beyond the structured confines of formal education, seeking the eternal truths that hovered just out of reach.

Scholastica, too, was an eager learner but her inclinations leaned more towards spiritual introspection and nurturing the soul through acts of devotion and piety. Their paths, while scholastically distinct, harmonized in a mutual longing to devote their lives to God. Their household, aware of the spiritual inclinations prefiguring in their children, fostered an environment where intellectual rigor and spiritual fervor were seen as two sides of the same divine coin.

The teachings of local clergy had an indelible impact on both siblings. These clergy, many of whom followed the austere path of early Christian ascetics, emphasized the importance of a life led by prayer, fasting, and community service. Young Benedict absorbed these teachings with a contemplative zeal that would later manifest in his creation of a monastic rule. Scholastica, imbued with an equally fervent spirit, found her calling in the nurturing roles traditionally ascribed to women but did so with a profound sense of divine purpose that transcended societal norms.

Visits to nearby monasteries and churches afforded Benedict and Scholastica real-world glimpses into the monastic life. These visits kindled within them a vision of communities bound by the shared pursuit of holiness, simplicity, and discipline. Observing the serene faces of monks and nuns, lost in prayer and divine meditation, the siblings internalized the beauty of a life consecrated to God.

Among the most pivotal early influences were the stories of martyrs and saints recounted by their educators and family members. Tales of unwavering faith amidst persecution resonated deeply with Benedict and Scholastica, instilling in them a steadfast courage and fortitude. Through these narratives, they learned that the path to righteousness often wove through trials and tribulations, yet it led to the ultimate glory of divine union.

Benedict was particularly moved by the writings of Saint Augustine, whose confessions and philosophical treatises offered profound reflections on the nature of sin, grace, and redemption. Scholastica, on the other hand, found solace in the lives of saintly women who had devoted themselves to Christ, such as Saint Agnes and Saint Cecilia. These inspirations would later crystallize into their own spiritual frameworks and practices, uniquely tailored yet unified in their underlying pursuit of divine love.

It's important to note the cultural and social milieu in which they were raised. The late antique period was a time of transformation and upheaval within the Roman Empire, yet it was also an era brimming with theological debates and ecclesiastical developments. The intellectual currents of Neoplatonism and early Christian theology interwove, offering a fertile ground for the young minds of Benedict and Scholastica to explore. This cultural tapestry provided them both a wealth of knowledge and a deep-seated conviction in the transformative power of spiritual discipline.

As they matured, both siblings faced choices that would set the trajectory of their lives. Benedict, witnessing the moral decay prevalent in urban Rome during his studies, felt a calling towards a more ascetic and disciplined path. Scholastica, though her journey took a different route, felt the same pull towards a life steeped in prayer and community-focused spirituality. These moments of decision were profoundly shaped by the lessons and influences of their early years in Nursia.

The educational aspects of their upbringing, though essential, were only a part of their formative experience. The landscape of Nursia, with its mountains, valleys, and streams, played a silent yet powerful role in nurturing their spirits. In the quietude of nature, they found a mirror reflecting the divine order and a sanctuary that amplified their inner contemplations. The natural world was not merely background; it was an integral part of the divine pedagogy that shaped their formative years.

In summary, the education and early influences of Saints Benedict and Scholastica were a harmonious blend of formal instruction, spiritual mentorship, and the silent yet profound lessons of nature. These formative years laid the foundation for their subsequent spiritual achievements and their enduring impact on Christian monasticism. Their lives remind us that true education is not confined to textbooks and classrooms but is a continuous process of engaging with the divine in all aspects of life, a process that molds the soul as much as the mind.

Founding of Monte Cassino

Nestled upon a hill in the quietude of the Italian countryside, Saint Benedict founded Monte Cassino in AD 529, amid the crumbling vestiges of a pagan temple dedicated to Apollo. This venerable site became a beacon of the Christian monastic tradition—a fortress of faith amidst a world teetering between chaos and divine order. Here, Benedict laid the cornerstone for his communal vision, blending sacred devotion with the dignity of labor, reflective of a harmonious celestial city amidst earthly tumult. Despite initial tribulations including opposition from local pagans and the challenge of fostering a new spiritual community, the monastery emerged as a resilient symbol of Christian renewal. Through prayer, work, and steadfast adherence to his nascent Rule, Benedict and his followers transformed Monte Cassino into a sanctuary of learning and piety, heralding a new era for Western monasticism.

Initial Challenges and Successes then, as dusk settled on Monte Cassino, Benedict marshaled his fledgling community, the nascent heartbeat of his monastic vision. To modern eyes, founding a monastery on a hilltop that had already seen Roman gods revered and war brought, may seem an almost quixotic endeavor. Yet it was precisely this interplay of the sacred and the profane that galvanized Benedict to carve out a sanctum for spiritual fortitude. His initial challenges mirrored the tribulations faced by any pioneering soul: suspicion from local inhabitants, the harshness of the natural environment, and the ever-looming specter of spiritual despondency among his brethren. From this crucible of trials, however, emerged the robust framework that would become the Benedictine Order.

Interestingly, one of the primary hurdles was assimilating men of varied dispositions and backgrounds into a harmonious monastic community. The human spirit, as capricious as it can be, found its alignment in Benedict's fledgling directives—the first echoes of his soon-to-be-celebrated Rule. It's a curious yet deeply telling facet of human nature that structure often begats freedom, especially freedom from the whims of one's own vices. Benedict's task was therefore as daunting as it was divine: he sought to yoke the flames of youthful zeal to the plough of disciplined spirituality without extinguishing their fervor.

Benedict's early successes were humble yet portentous. When the first small group of monks gathered, sharing in the rhythms of work and prayer, the foundations of monastic order crystallized almost imperceptibly. The first chant of the Divine Office resonated in the still air of Monte Cassino like an amen to inaugural prayers. As in all great enterprises, it was these seemingly mundane yet profoundly symbolic acts that began to weave the tapestry of monastic life. It is in enduring the scorching summer heat and icy winter winds alike, that the monks found their sanctified balance.

The turning point came through trials that were not merely spiritual but also corporeal. Rascal bands, sometimes lingering remnants of pagan sects, eyed the establishment with a mixture of curiosity and veiled hostility. It is as though the sacred space evoked in them an existential challenge. The crucible of conflict clarified purpose, reinforcing the resolve of the monks. Each moment of tension, potentially disastrous, transmuted into resolve forged in the fellowship of shared danger. Remarkably, Benedict's faith in divine providence coalesced this external opposition into a stronger internal unity, the first true success forged from adversity.

Material resources posed another formidable challenge. The scarcity of food and the paucity of shelter rendered day-to-day existence a severe regimen that only the most devoted could endure. Yet, necessity, often the sternest of pedagogues, ushered innovation. Guided by Benedict's nascent principles, the monks engaged in pioneering agricultural and artisan endeavors. The burgeoning community's needs gave birth to new forms of sustainable work. Through tilling unyielding soil and erecting makeshift shelters, they shaped both the environment and their spirits. Over time, Monte Cassino transformed from a desolate hillto one radiating serene fecundity.

One significant factor in combating these early material struggles was the gradual but vital support of local benefactors. As the monk's reputation for piety and industriousness spread, so too did the sympathy of the local Christian populace. Donations of lands, seeds, and livestock, while modest at first, began to trickle into the community. Herein lay another triumph amid the trials: the delicate, unspoken contract between the monks and the laypeople began to form, a partnership integral to the long-term stability of Monte Cassino. This symbiotic relationship foreshadowed the role that Benedictine monasteries would come to play in medieval European society as anchors of both spiritual and agrarian life.

Success also emerged in the area of spiritual discipline. Benedict's early monks were not seasoned ascetics; many were neophytes to the monastic life. The challenge was to instill in them a rhythm of prayer, reflection, and labor that was demanding yet attainable. Daily routines became the crucibles for spiritual transformation. Through shared liturgy, communal meals, and a common rule, Benedict's vision of "ora et labora" took practical shape. What began as a guideline slowly but inexorably metamorphosed into a way of life as seamless as it was sanctified. The initial struggles to maintain consistency and devotion turned in time into successes marking the genuine growth of their collective spirituality.

One cannot underestimate the impact of external events on internal formation. Historical forces aligned in unimaginable ways, creating both obstacles and opportunities. Those early years were marked by political uncertainties that colored the entire Mediterranean world. Amid this chaos, the monastery provided an island of tranquility and spiritual sustenance. Every successful resolution of conflict, every reclaimed patch of farmland, and every deepening prayer gathered the vitality of purpose. The joys, though muted and often mingled with sorrow, built a reservoir of fortitude that etched Benedictine life indelibly into the fabric of the monks' existence.

Undoubtedly, Benedict's steadfastness was indispensable to these initial successes. His leadership mirrored the stoic resilience of a guiding star, profoundly affecting the trajectory of those around him. Through stories handed down, we understand that it was Benedict's unwavering faith that often rallied his disheartened brethren. His ability to see beyond the immediate hardships and envision a thriving spiritual community allowed him to instill hope even during the direst days. This sense of an overarching divine purpose was compellingly persuasive, cementing not only his role as founder but as a father in faith.

As we journey through time's corridors, it's evident that Benedict's initial challenges and successes laid the cornerstone for a lasting spiritual edifice. What was once a tentative gathering of souls on a desolate hill morphed into an enduring spiritual lineage, resonating through centuries. These foundational struggles and subsequent triumphs did more than ensure the survival of Monte Cassino; they adorned it with the sanctity of experience, a testament to both temporal endurance and divine grace. Here was the living proof that divine order could manifest through human effort, framed by Benedict's inspired yet pragmatic vision.

Chapter 3: The Rule of Saint Benedict

The Rule of Saint Benedict, meticulously crafted in the 6th century, stands as both a spiritual guideline and a pragmatic framework for monastic life, balancing prayer, work, and communal living in a harmonious dance. It's imbued with an egalitarian spirit, urging the abbot to be a loving shepherd and the monks to obediently follow, embodying virtues like humility, silence, and self-denial. Far from a mere set of instructions, the Rule creates a utopian vision of a cohesive community bound by divine love, where even the smallest tasks hold spiritual significance. The intricate web of precepts and daily disciplines fosters a serene yet industrious life, where each monk's sanctified labor contributes to the collective good. It invites adherents to seek God through the routine—transforming the ordinary into the extraordinary and the temporal into the eternal. Benedict's wisdom thus transcends time, offering not just a historical artifact but a perpetual beacon guiding monastic and lay communities alike through the labyrinth of spiritual and earthly existence.

Principles and Precepts

The "Rule of Saint Benedict," often seen as a manual for monastic living, is a guiding light that transcends its immediate historical context. Central to this revered document are the principles and precepts that articulate not only the discipline but also the philosophy underpinning Benedictine life. Here, the fabric of monasticism is stitched with threads of humility, obedience, and community, weaving a tapestry that has shaped Christian monasticism for centuries.

At the core, Saint Benedict emphasizes the virtue of humility. Humility, in the Benedictine sense, is not simply about self-abasement but a profound recognition of one's place in a larger divine order. This principle draws heavily from biblical sources, urging monks to understand their own limitations while simultaneously recognizing the grandeur of God's creation. In this context, humility is a path toward spiritual enlightenment, a means to align oneself more closely with divine will. It's a fundamental posture of the soul, influencing actions, thoughts, and relationships within the monastic community.

Obedience is another cornerstone of the Rule. Derived from Latin "oboedire" which means "to listen," obedience in Benedictine life is an act of attentive listening to the will of God, often articulated through the abbot, the community leader. This principle is radical in its demand for self-surrender, where the monk's personal desires are subjugated to the needs and directives of the community. This form of obedience is not blind; it is imbued with discernment and awareness, fostering a disciplined and harmonious environment within the monastery.

Community life is indispensable in the Rule. The monastic community is envisioned as a family under the abbot's guidance, who acts as a loving father. The Rule establishes a balance between collective and individual needs, designing a structure that supports communal prayer, shared work, and mutual support. The common life is a crucible for spiritual growth, where monks learn to live in harmony with one another, mirroring the relational aspects of Christian teaching. It's not merely a logistical arrangement but a spiritual exercise in love and charity.

Silence and mindfulness are also central principles in the Rule of Saint Benedict. Silence is not the mere absence of speech but an active, contemplative practice that encourages mindfulness and introspection. The purpose of silence is to foster an atmosphere conducive to prayer and reflection, helping monks to focus their hearts and minds on divine matters. In a world full of distractions, this principle remains profoundly counter-cultural and deeply enriching.

The Rule also emphasizes the importance of stability, which anchors the monk physically and spiritually to a particular community and place. This commitment to stability is seen as a vow, symbolizing a long-term dedication to spiritual growth in a specific context. The principle teaches resilience and fidelity, encouraging monks to confront and work through difficulties rather than fleeing them. It's an enduring commitment to both the monastic community and the individual's spiritual journey.

Another critical aspect is the integration of prayer and work, known as "Ora et Labora." The Rule underscores that these two activities are not mutually exclusive but interconnected aspects of monastic life. Prayer sanctifies work, and work becomes an act of prayer. This holistic approach encourages monks to see labor—whether manual or intellectual—as a form of worship, imbuing even the most mundane tasks with spiritual significance. This principle promotes a balanced and integrated life, where the sacred and the secular coexist harmoniously.

The Rule also outlines what can be termed as "the economy of charity." This principle posits that everything within the monastery should serve the common good. Possessions are held in common, and monks are encouraged to practice generosity toward each other. This communal sharing reflects the early Christian communities described in the Acts of the Apostles, fostering a spirit of compassion and mutual support. By prioritizing collective well-being over individual wealth, the Rule creates an environment where material concerns are secondary to spiritual and communal harmony.

The principle of discretion holds a unique place in Benedictine spirituality. Discretion here refers to the quality of discernment and balanced judgment. It's a counterweight to zeal and excess, promoting a measured approach to monastic disciplines and practices. This principle ensures that the Rule is adaptable to individual circumstances and needs, preventing rigid legalism. Discretion, therefore, is the lens through which the Rule's directives are interpreted and applied, making it a living document rather than a static code.

Benedict's Rule also offers a comprehensive vision of leadership, centered around the figure of the abbot. Leadership, according to Benedict, should be marked by wisdom, fairness, and compassion. The abbot is seen not as a tyrant but as a shepherd, guiding the community with love and discernment. This principle underscores the importance of servant leadership, where authority is exercised through service and humility rather than domination. It's a model that has influenced countless spiritual and secular leaders throughout history.

The Rule's principles and precepts also extend to the care and inclusion of the weakest members of the community. Benedict explicitly instructs that the sick, the elderly, and guests should receive special attention and care. This principle of hospitality and care for the vulnerable exemplifies the Christian values of love and service, making the monastery a place of refuge and compassion. It's an embodiment of the Gospel mandate to care for "the least of these" and a testament to the Rule's enduring social relevance.

In essence, the principles and precepts of the Rule of Saint Benedict provide a roadmap for a life oriented toward God, community, and personal growth. They form the bedrock of Benedictine monasticism, creating a spiritual framework that has endured for over 1,500 years. These principles speak to the deep human longing for order, purpose, and communion, offering timeless wisdom for both monastic and secular contexts.

Through its emphasis on humility, obedience, community, silence, stability, prayer, work, charity, discretion, leadership, and care for the vulnerable, the Rule remains a profound and practical guide for spiritual living. Its principles continue to resonate today, not just in monasteries but in the hearts of all who seek a life of deeper meaning and divine connection. The Rule of Saint Benedict, with its rich tapestry of precepts, serves as a perennial beacon, guiding souls toward a harmonious and holy life.

Daily Life and Discipline

The "Rule of Saint Benedict," a foundational text for Western monasticism, mandates a structured, disciplined, and spiritually-oriented daily life. This sacred guideline emphasizes a balance of prayer, work, and rest, creating a rhythm that fosters both individual sanctity and communal harmony. Benedict's vision was not merely for an individual way of living but for a societal microcosm that reflected divine order on Earth.

Daily activities within the monastery begin with the ringing of the bell in pre-dawn hours, calling the monks to the first communal prayer of the day, known as Vigils. The early rise signifies an immediate offering of the mind and heart to God, a symbolic act of prioritizing spiritual duties above the comfort of rest. Following Vigils, the monks engage in Lectio Divina (divine reading), a meditative and reflective practice aimed at deepening their understanding of sacred scriptures. The readings are not confined to biblical texts alone but also include writings from the church fathers and other spiritual luminaries.

A monk's day pivots around the canonical hours, structured times for communal prayer, which provide spiritual checkpoints throughout the day. Each session, including Lauds, Prime, Terce, Sext, None, Vespers, and Compline, acts as a reminder of divine omnipresence and the monk's mission. This rhythmic intermingling of prayer and labor embodies the Benedictine motto "Ora et Labora" (pray and work), reinforcing the integrated spirituality that defines the Rule. While prayer anchors the monastic schedule, work is equally enshrined as an act of worship.

In the Benedictine tradition, labor is sacred and essential. The Rule allocates manual tasks that vary from agricultural work to transcribing manuscripts. These tasks are not relegated to mere subsistence activities but are considered pathways to humility and divine service. Benedictine monasteries often thrived as self-sustaining communities where each member's contribution, no matter how menial, was valued as part of the collective offering to God. It is through this lens that mundane chores are transformed into acts of devotion.

Discipline extends beyond structured activities; it permeates the monastic lifestyle itself. Abstaining from excesses, monks practice moderation and renunciation, facilitating a life unburdened by the distractions of materialism. Meals within the monastery are simple, taken in silence while a designated monk delivers readings from edifying texts. This practice encourages mindful eating and reinforces the spiritual dimension of every aspect of life.

The Rule also prescribes periods of rest, acknowledging the necessity of corporeal renewal. Benedict understood that physical well-being directly influences spiritual fervor and community stability. Therefore, appropriate time is allotted for sleep, recreation, and personal reflection. In such balance lies the secret to sustained monastic life, reflecting a divine equilibrium between body and soul.

Social harmony within the monastery is meticulously curated through codified interactions and communal responsibilities. The Benedictine vow of obedience is paramount, requiring monks to submit to the abbot's authority as Christ's representative. This vow underscores a cruciform humility, aligning personal will with collective needs and spiritual objectives. Each monk is expected to act with obedience, respect, and love towards one another, fostering a fraternal atmosphere grounded in common values.

Silence plays an essential role in daily discipline, functioning as a gateway to contemplation and inner peace. The Rule mandates periods of silence, creating a milieu conducive to spiritual introspection and divine connection. While rigorous, the silent regimen is not stifling; it is interspersed with spoken prayers and chants, striking a harmonious balance between vocal expression and reflective stillness.

Fraternity is further nurtured through regular Chapter meetings, where monks gather to discuss communal affairs, confess faults, and receive spiritual instruction. These meetings are a testament to the egalitarian spirit within the Rule, offering a platform for transparent communication and collective discernment. The abbot, though holding final authority, is expected to listen and consider the insights and concerns of his brethren, reinforcing mutual accountability and respect.

Moreover, the Rule is insistent on the care and inclusion of novices, juvenile monks, and any who are weak or infirm. This mandate for compassionate governance extends beyond mere hospitality; it demands that the stronger monks bear with the infirmities of the weak with utmost patience and love. Benedict's vision here is utopian in that it calls for a community where mutual support and understanding create an environment of spiritual growth and human flourishing.

Furthermore, the Rule's discipline encompasses a corrective dimension. Punitive measures for transgressions are designed not to ostracize but to rehabilitate. Monks who err are met with corrective actions aimed at restoring them to communal and spiritual integrity. The emphasis on correction rather than punishment underscores a deep commitment to each monk's sanctity and the overall health of the community.

The Rule of Saint Benedict, in stipulating such an encompassing daily discipline, crafts not merely a religious regimen but a way of life aspirational in its adherence to divine order. It breathes life into ancient wisdom, elevating mundane existence into an overarching spiritual odyssey. For those who embrace its rhythms, the Rule offers a lifelong pilgrimage toward holiness, contextualized within the supportive embrace of the monastic community.

This disciplined life, though demanding, attracts souls yearning for divine intimacy and communal harmony. Its ancient structure still resonates in the modern era, revealing that the truths encapsulated within the Rule transcend time and usher adherents toward a life marked by holiness, humility, and service. Ultimately, the "Daily Life and Discipline" as prescribed in the Rule of Saint Benedict encapsulates a utopian quest for spiritual and communal perfection, laying the groundwork for a disciplined yet profoundly fulfilling monastic existence.

Chapter 4: Saint Scholastica: Sister and Spiritual Companion

Amid the burgeoning dawn of Benedictine monasticism, Saint Scholastica emerges as a radiant beacon of spiritual companionship and unwavering devotion. Her early life, marked by an intrinsic call to sacred service, paralleled that of her brother, Saint Benedict. Together, they wove an intricate tapestry of faith and familial bonds that transcended the temporal realm. Scholastica's presence was not merely that of a sibling, but of a profound spiritual counterpart whose shared vision furthered the ideals of monastic life. In her acts of gentle wisdom and devout prayer, the seeds of Benedictine spirituality found fertile ground. Her memorable encounter with Benedict, where divine intervention turned a sibling dialogue into a night-long divine colloquy, serves as an allegorical manifestation of saintly perseverance and divine favor. Scholastica thus stands as a testament to the transformative power of spiritual kinship, echoing through the corridors of monastic history, inspiring generations in their pursuit of a life dedicated to piety and communal harmony.

Early Life and Vocation

In the serene hills of Nursia, within the foothills of the Sibylline Mountains, was born a pair of siblings whose destinies would become entwined with the spiritual contours of Christian monasticism. Scholastica and her twin brother, Benedict, emerged into a world marked by the struggle for moral fortitude amidst the decline of the Western Roman Empire. Their family, one of noble lineage, was imbued with the ideals of Christian virtue and Roman civic duty. However, it was Scholastica whose pure and unblemished faith would become the cornerstone of her life and mission.

Even in their youngest years, Scholastica and Benedict bore witness to the fracturing world around them and the conflicting tides of secular and spiritual callings. It is said that Scholastica showed an early predilection for piety, a stirring of the soul that distinguished her from her peers. In the domestic sanctity of their family estate, she absorbed the prayers, hymns, and sacred rituals that would come to define her spiritual journey. Her devotion was unwavering, a nascent spiritual fire that flickered but never diminished.

Education in the early Christian world was not merely an intellectual pursuit but a spiritual one. Scholastica's learning began at home, where her parents provided instruction in the Scriptures, Latin, and the rudiments of classical knowledge. Through these teachings, Scholastica found in the sacred annals and ancient texts not just words, but the whispers of God calling her to a life set apart. This learning was not confined to the written word alone; the oral traditions of the saints and the lived example of their virtues profoundly shaped her understanding of faith.

As the nascent Christian communities around them flourished and faltered under the weight of external pressures, Scholastica's vocation grew steadily and surely. She was drawn to a life of sanctity and prayer, perhaps influenced deeply by her brother's similar devotion. Benedict, too, discerned the muddled call of the divine amidst the chaos, setting forth his path towards the establishment of monastic life. Their respective vocations, while unique, were symbiotically linked, each reinforcing and illuminating the path of the other.

Scholastica's earliest brushes with monastic life likely came through her proximity to Benedict's spiritual endeavors. The ideals encapsulated in the communities forming around her brother's teachings were a lodestar for her blossoming vocation. Yet, it was clear from the onset that Scholastica's journey was her own, distinct yet inherently connected to her brother's. She sought the divine through the contemplative silences of the cloister, the rhythmic cadence of the Psalms, and the communal bonds formed in shared faith.

While historical records of Scholastica's early life may be sparse, these lacunae allow us to consider the depth of her inner life. Her spirituality was not one of grand gestures but of quiet, resolute faith. The contours of her vocation were shaped in the moments of silent prayer, the simplicity of daily devotions, and the steadfast commitment to live out the principles of her newfound monastic community. This was a life marked by an intimate relationship with God, one that flourished in the solitude of her heart even as it prepared to embrace community.

One must not overlook the allegorical significance of the twinship of Scholastica and Benedict. It symbolizes the dual aspects of the spiritual journey: action and contemplation, community and solitude, masculinity and femininity. Scholastica's pathway to holiness complemented and contrasted with Benedict's, emphasizing the holistic nature of Christian sanctification. Her vocation, like a delicate thread, wove itself into the larger tapestry of Benedictine monasticism, enriching it with her unique spiritual insights and feminine grace.

Scholastica's eventual founding of a religious community for women, parallel to Benedict's establishment at Monte Cassino, was a natural extension of her early life and inclinations. The call to lead and nurture a sisterhood in faith mirrored the nurturing grace she no doubt practiced in her familial and spiritual relationships. The establishment of her community was not merely an administrative act but the birth of a living, breathing organism of faith, where Scholastica's formative experiences merged with her divine calling.

Her leadership was deeply maternal, marked by a nurturing spirit and an unwavering commitment to the spiritual and temporal well-being of her charges. The principles and precepts she embraced and imparted echoed the larger Benedictine ideals but were also suffused with her unique sensitivity and insight. Her community thrived on the balance between ora et labora, the symbiotic relationship between prayer and work that core tenet of Benedictine life. Scholastica's vocation was thus the embodiment of her early desires and the culmination of her lifelong communion with the divine.

Even in the light of her profound spiritual achievements, the essence of Scholastica's early life remains a testament to the beauty of silent dedication and unwavering faith. Her early years, though not festooned with grandiose narratives or miraculous interventions, were the fertile ground from which her profound spirituality grew. It was in the quiet moments of her youth, in the devotional practices and familial bonds, that the seeds of her vocation were sown. Scholastica's legacy, therefore, is one of humble beginnings transformed into a life of holy purpose and divine fulfillment.

The vocational journey of Scholastica invites us to reflect upon the quiet, often hidden, moments of our own lives where divine callings may whisper to us. Her story underscores the significance of rejecting complacency and seeking the sacred in the seemingly mundane rhythms of daily life. Scholastica's life was a gradual but steadfast ascent towards spiritual enlightenment, a journey marked by the milestones of faith, love, and unwavering commitment to God's will.

As we ponder the early life and vocation of Saint Scholastica, we recognize in her a mirror reflecting both the struggles and triumphs of all those who seek to live a life devoted to the divine. Her story serves as a poignant reminder of the transformative power of faith and the profound impact of a life lived in devoted service. Scholastica, in her silent dedication, offers us a paradigm of holiness that transcends time and place, inviting us all to enter into a deeper communion with the eternal.

Relationship with Saint Benedict

Saint Scholastica, adorned in the veils of piety and profound spiritual resonance, stands as a unique figure in the annals of Christian history, primarily because of her indelible bond with her twin brother, Saint Benedict. This relationship wasn't merely one of blood but of soul and spirit, deeply intertwined through their mutual pursuit of religious asceticism and divine engagement. Their interconnected journey offers insight into the profound impact they had upon each other, and subsequently, the shape of early monastic life.

Born in Nursia around the year 480, they shared not only familial ties but a symbiotic spiritual quest that would set the foundation for Much of Western monasticism. The bond started in their shared upbringing, steeped in the values of early Christian virtues and the pursuit of holiness. Despite the societal norms of the time, which often placed women in subsidiary roles, Scholastica's relationship with Benedict was one of mutual respect and spiritual equality. They nurtured each other's faith, forming a foundation that supported their eventual ventures into monasticism.

One can trace the physical and metaphysical paths they took. While Saint Benedict became renowned for his establishment of Monte Cassino and the formulation of the Benedictine Rule, Scholastica pursued her vocation with an equally fervent devotion, though in a less documented manner. The spiritual gravity of their relationship can be seen in the exchanges they shared; it was deep, contemplative, and filled with a shared zeal for divine understanding.

Their interactions were minimal yet profoundly impactful. Benedict's strict adherence to his Rule, which emphasized balance, prayer, and work, often mirrored the quiet, contemplative life Scholastica led. Despite the physical distance, they maintained a spiritual connection through letters and occasional visits. These visits were not just familial reunions but spiritual councils, where they would discuss theological ideas and the nuances of their respective practices.

The most celebrated of their meetings, chronicled by Pope Gregory the Great in his Dialogues, portrays a serene but decisive portrayal of Scholastica's spiritual depth. During one of Benedict's annual visits to her monastery, Scholastica, sensing her impending death, implored her brother to stay longer to discuss divine matters. Benedict, adhering strictly to his Rule, refused. What followed was a poignant act of divine intervention: Scholastica prayed, and a fierce storm erupted, preventing Benedict from departing. This episode is not merely a testament to Scholastica's spiritual fervor but also an embodiment of their relationship—one that balanced stringent adherence to religious rules with profound, heartfelt devotion.

This episode has been interpreted allegorically to represent the eternal wrestling between law and love, discipline and grace. Scholastica's unwavering faith and her triumphant prayer over natural elements reflect the power of sincere piety and divine intercession. It underscores a thematic element present in many religious texts: love and faith, when pure, can transcend even the most rigid structures. Her victory in this instance is a quiet yet potent reminder of the sanctity embraced by both siblings.

Their interdependence also served a greater purpose: it acted as a beacon for the early Christian community, demonstrating the harmonization of gender roles within a religious context. Scholastica's influence on Benedict, paired with her dedication to the monastic life, provided a model for the integration of women into these spiritual narratives. Their relationship illustrated that spiritual wisdom was not confined by gender but was a shared pursuit towards divine living.

After Scholastica's death, Benedict's reaction further illuminates the depth of their bond. According to tradition, Benedict saw her soul ascend to heaven in the form of a dove. This vision reaffirmed the sanctity of her life and their spiritual connection. He insisted that her body be interred in the tomb he had prepared for himself, symbolizing their inseparable bond even in death. Their joint resting place became a site of veneration, illustrating the enduring nature of their spiritual kinship.

The legacy of their relationship continued to influence Benedictine practices and the broader Christian tradition. Scholastica, through her exemplary piety and her role as a spiritual equal to Benedict, helped shape the perception of women in the monastic world. The narrative of their connection offers a profound reflection on how familial bonds can transcend earthly existence, forging pathways to divine unity.

The mutual support and shared aspirations of Scholastica and Benedict serve as an inspirational narrative within the wider context of Christian monasticism. Their relationship wasn't just a matter of blood; it was a testament to shared spiritual pathways, reinforcing the idea that the pursuit of divine understanding is enriched by companionship. Scholastica's unwavering faith and her influence on Benedict are immortalized in the annals of history, serving as an enduring example of spiritual collaboration.

By exploring their relationship, we gain insight into the intricate dynamics of early monastic life and the role of relational bonds in the pursuit of sanctity. Scholastica, through her quiet but powerful example, established a legacy intertwined with Benedict's, reminding us that spiritual guidance often comes from unexpected sources and that the journey towards divine grace is a shared one, enriched by mutual respect and unwavering devotion.

In conclusion, the relationship between Saint Scholastica and Saint Benedict encapsulates a harmonious blending of love, discipline, and faith. Their interactions reveal a profound mutual respect and dedication to their spiritual vocations. This bond not only shaped their lives but also left a lasting imprint on the Christian monastic tradition, offering a model of spiritual companionship that transcends time and continues to inspire.

Chapter 5: Gender Roles in Benedictine Monasticism

In the hallowed rhythms of Benedictine monasticism, gender roles were both distinct and harmonious, each complementing the other in the pursuit of divine order. Men and women, guided by the Rule of Saint Benedict, found their paths diverging yet converging in spiritual purpose. Saint Scholastica, revered as Benedict's sister and equal in sanctity, played an indelible role in shaping the contours of female monastic life. Her influence shone not merely as a mirror to her brother's legacy but as a beacon in her own right, encapsulating the Christian ideal of contemplation balanced with action. The monastic life offered women an alternative to traditional societal roles, providing them a sacred space for intellectual and spiritual growth. Yet, it also reinforced certain medieval gender norms, delineating parameters within which women's influence flourished, largely through communal prayer, teaching, and nurturing the spiritual well-being of their communities. This duality of liberation and restraint crafted a unique mosaic of gender dynamics within the tranquil cloisters, echoing through the centuries as a testament to the profound yet nuanced interplay between masculine and feminine spiritual engagements.

The Role of Women in Monastic Life

Women in Benedictine monasticism, epitomized by the figure of Saint Scholastica, embraced a role both complementary to and distinct from their male counterparts. As spiritual matriarchs, they cultivated a life of prayer, discipline, and communal labor, mirroring the ideals set by Saint Benedict but adapted to the unique needs of female monastic communities. Their contributions went beyond spiritual devotion; they became custodians of knowledge, skilled artisans, and beacons of charity. In an era marked by strict gender roles, these women carved out a sacred space where they could nurture their spiritual selves and serve their communities. The duality of their existence illustrated an allegorical battleground of utopian aspirations and dystopian realities, revealing the profound capacity for sanctity within the bounds of societal constraints. By fostering environments of spiritual growth and scholarship, they created microcosms of divine order, echoing the celestial harmony envisioned by their male counterparts while navigating the terrestrial challenges distinct to their sex. Their legacies, interwoven with tales of mysticism and piety, illuminate the indomitable spirit of the women who, within the cloistered walls of monastic life, found a path to transcendence.

Saint Scholastica's Influence bridges two significant paradigms within the Benedictine tradition: the melding of monastic ideals and the unique spiritual lens brought forth by women. Scholastica, often overshadowed by her more famous twin brother, Saint Benedict, was undeniable in her impact. Her life offers a compelling illustration of how female monasticism shaped, complemented, and at times, challenged the early frameworks of Benedictine spirituality.

Born into the same noble family as Benedict, Saint Scholastica imbibed the rich ecclesiastical traditions of their upbringing. Despite the epoch's limitations on women's roles in religious settings, Scholastica carved her own luminous path, mirroring yet distinct from her brother's. Her dedication to spiritual life was unwavering, marked by an indomitable spirit that bent orthodoxy to the contours of feminine experience. This nuanced approach led to the flourishing of female monasticism, offering a vital counterbalance in a predominantly male dominion.

The episode that most captivatingly encapsulates Scholastica's influence is the famous narrative of her last meeting with Benedict. Seeking additional time in prayerful conversation with her brother, Scholastica implored divine assistance to prevent his departure. The ensuing storm trapped Benedict at her convent, and it's said that she joyfully attributed this event to her deep faith. This story, while simple, profoundly conveys the flowing grace and spiritual potency attributed to Scholastica, further demonstrating her intimate relationship with the divine—a relationship through which she subtly rewrote the monastic narratives of her time.

Her impact did not rest solely on miraculous episodes. Scholastica's convents operated as havens where wisdom and piety thrived, echoing the principles laid down in her brother's Rule but adapted to the sensibilities and necessities of her female followers. These convents became places of learned refuge where women could live out their vocations with dignity and purpose. Scholastica's discerning leadership illuminated pathways that bridged gender divides, often harnessing the Rule's ideals of balance, harmony, and community to craft environments where female monasticism could prosper authentically.

Moreover, Scholastica's influence lived on in the nuns who followed her. Through oral traditions and the perpetuation of her values, she inspired generations of women who chose the cloistered life. Her legacy is evidenced by the countless female monastic communities that arose, bearing witness to her model of devoted spirituality, cloaked in the practicalities of day-to-day religious life. These communities became custodians not just of faith but also of culture and knowledge, safeguarding and transmitting these treasures through turbulent times.

In a broader allegorical sense, Scholastica's influence can be seen as a beacon of inclusivity within the Benedictine tradition. Her life serves as a testament to the spiritual equality that transcends human-imposed boundaries. Scholastica lived out the Pauline ideal that "in Christ, there is neither male nor female," echoing a utopian vision of spiritual parity and collaborative ministry. Her story and its embedded values have inspired a quieter yet resilient current of egalitarian thought that continues to ripple through the halls of monastic study and practice.

Adding to her mettle, Scholastica exemplified a lived theology that emphasized relational spirituality. Her symbiotic relationship with her brother becomes a paradigm for understanding the confluence of male and female spiritual energies within the monastic ideal. Their mutual influence underscored that the solitary pursuit of holiness, though paramount, is enriched immeasurably by the communion shared within the community and between genders. Through Scholastica, a vision of the contemplative life emerged that harmonized the masculine and feminine, the austere and the compassionate.

Further illustrating her profound impact, the Benedictine nuns under Scholastica's aegis became essential players in the medieval educational and healthcare landscapes. They extended charity to the poor and ill, embodying the practical outworking of monastic values in everyday life. These services provided an ethical and spiritual framework that furthered societal stability and moral consciousness amidst the vicissitudes of medieval Europe. Such efforts illuminate the broader societal influence of Scholastica's spiritual leadership, extending well beyond the cloister's walls into the very fabric of community life.

Saint Scholastica's spiritual wisdom also profoundly influenced the liturgical practices within Benedictine communities. Her emphasis on the prayerful immersion into the rhythms of divine office and her specific devotion to specific prayers brought a distinct flavor to the liturgical life of Benedictine nuns. This devotion became a distinctive marker of identity for these communities, reflecting Scholastica's personal ardor for intimate communion with God. This engaged form of spirituality underpinned the nuns' daily routines, reinforcing a spirituality that was fervently alive and deeply rooted in the exigencies of their daily dedication.

Analyzing Scholastica's influence through a more allegorical lens, she can be seen as a maternal figure embodying the Church's nurturing and inclusive potential. Her convents symbolized safe havens, reflecting a spiritual utopia where simplicity, order, and grace reigned. Such spaces offered refuge and spiritual renewal to those weary of the world's burdens, establishing a microcosm of divine order amid temporal chaos. Scholastica's life thus becomes an allegory—a narrative that transcends its time, carrying timeless principles of openness, balance, and holy receptivity. Her very existence in the annals of Benedictine tradition provides a spiritual counter-narrative that highlights the fecundity of female monastic leadership.

In the tapestry of Benedictine history, Scholastica's influence is akin to a golden thread—delicate yet indispensable, subtle yet shining brightly through centuries. It mirrors a utopian ideal of utilizing monastic virtues as tools for bridging divides, fostering unified communities radiating divine charity and wisdom. Scholastica's life exemplifies not only a dedicated pursuit of personal holiness but also a visionary inclusivity that wove her influence into the interstices of monastic and societal norms.

Saint Scholastica's legacy continues to inspire, indicating that her influence endures in the living tradition of Benedictine monasticism. Her nuanced vision expanded the Benedictine ethos to embrace the full spectrum of human and divine possibility, creating a paradigm of holiness that transcended gender, time, and space. Rather than existing as a mere appendage to her brother's renown, Scholastica's influence manifests as an integrated and vital force, shaping the very essence of Benedictine life and spirituality. Her story offers an enduring testament to the transformative power embedded in the humble, disciplined, and prayerful life, inviting future generations to heed her spiritual cues.

Chapter 6: Spiritual Practices and Devotions

The spiritual practices and devotions embedded in the lives of Saints Benedict and Scholastica form the bedrock of Benedictine monasticism, weaving a tapestry of prayer, contemplation, and ritual that transcends time. Central to their spiritual regimen were the structured hours of the Divine Office, where the day was punctuated by moments of sacred pause, echoing the rhythm of creation itself. Their devotion wasn't merely an act of piety but a profound communion with the divine, fostering a utopian harmony within the monastic community. With an unwavering commitment to ora et labora (prayer and work), they not only sought personal sanctity but also envisioned a society shaped by spiritual discipline. Through their devout practices, Saints Benedict and Scholastica left an indelible mark on the spiritual landscape, guiding countless souls toward a contemplative life that balances the material with the transcendent.

Prayer and Contemplation

In the hallowed halls of monastic life, prayer and contemplation stand as twin pillars upholding the very essence of Benedictine spirituality. Saint Benedict, with the wisdom of an architect of souls, meticulously wove these practices into the daily rhythm of monastic life, fostering a sanctuary where the divine and human intersect. The journey of prayer, enveloped in the sacred hours, guides the monks and nuns into a continual dialogue with the Divine, while contemplation transforms the mind, leading it beyond the ephemeral to touch the eternal. The essence of Benedict's vision, shared and nurtured by his sister Saint Scholastica, resides in this unwavering commitment to spiritual communion. This mutual dedication reveals not only the depths of their personal sanctity but also a blueprint for transcendence that continues to inspire the faithful and intrigue historians. The seamless blending of labor and audacious devotion represents a utopia for the soul, a place where the trials of the earthly realm meet the promise of heavenly peace, resonating through centuries as a testament to their enduring legacy.

The Hours and Daily Offices form the rhythmic backbone of Benedictine monastic life, weaving a tapestry of prayer and contemplation that connects the earthly realm with the divine. Within the sacred precincts of monasteries, marked by the tolling of bells and whispers of ancient chants, these structured intervals transform daily existence into an ongoing sacrament. More than mere routines, they epitomize a relentless dedication to a life of spiritual discipline and community. Whether waking before dawn or retiring after the day's labor, each monk engages in a perpetual dialogue with God, an ethereal symphony composed of both individual reflection and collective worship.

The core of these devotions lies in the Liturgy of the Hours, also known as the Divine Office. Saint Benedict, drawing upon early Christian traditions and possibly influenced by the structure of Roman civic life, meticulously organized these into eight canonical hours. Each 'hour' isn't a literal 60-minute period but a designated time for specific prayers and psalms. They begin with Matins (or Vigils) in the dead of night, moving through Lauds at dawn, followed by Prime, Terce, Sext, None, Vespers at evening, and finally Compline before the silence of night. Through these demarcated times, Benedictine spirituality aspires to fulfill the Apostle Paul's call to "pray without ceasing."

Matins, often considered the spiritual watchtower of the night, covers a thematic expanse from mortality to the anticipation of eternal life. This period of nocturnal vigil is not just about prayer; it's an embodiment of the soul's longing to transcend earthly bounds, seeking a foretaste of heavenly light in the depths of darkness. Matins invites the monks into a contemplative wrestling with scripture, hymns, and readings, encouraging an awareness that, even in the silence of night, God's presence remains steadfast. The night watch thus becomes a time of heightened spiritual awareness, a liminal space teetering between the known and the mystical.

At dawn, Lauds inaugurates the day with praises that merge the new light with divine radiance. The tranquil yet jubilant nature of Lauds underscores gratitude and renewal, symbolizing a resurrection with each morning's light. Here, the Benedictine philosophy captures a potent allegory of Christ's resurrection, as each dawn breaks the metaphorical chains of night and darkness. Focusing on psalms and prayers filled with themes of praise and creation, Lauds becomes both an anchor and a sail, grounding the monastic community while propelling them towards their daily spiritual endeavors.

Prime, Terce, Sext, and None occur at the transitional points of the day: morning, mid-morning, noon, and mid-afternoon, respectively. These minor hours are moments of refocusing, gently nudging monastic hearts and minds back to their divine purpose amidst daily tasks. Prime, the first of these daylight prayers, traditionally marked the beginning of one's active responsibilities, binding spiritual intention with physical action. The hours of Terce, Sext, and None, smaller in scale but equally significant, carve out sacred spaces within the mundane flow of time. Through them, the monks are reminded that God is present not only in overt acts of worship but also in the silent labor of daily life.

As evening falls, Vespers, often one of the most beautiful offices, signifies the completion of the day's work with hymns of thanksgiving. The golden hues of twilight blending with chanted psalms create a serene atmosphere of gratitude and reflection. Vespers encapsulates the comfort of rest after toil, a communal offering of the day's fruits and a time to seek divine grace for any failures. The evening light, casting long shadows across the serene monastic enclosures, symbolizes both an end and a prelude – bridging the day that was with the night that will be.

Compline, the final office of the day, is steeped in themes of protection and peace. This night prayer seeks divine guardianship through the dark hours, invoking a unique sense of closure. It's a time for monks to acknowledge their human vulnerabilities and to place their trust in God's perpetual vigilance. The simplicity and repetitiveness of the prayers and psalms in Compline help to calm the mind, evoking a collective sigh that releases the anxieties of the day. In this sacred silence, monks prepare their souls for the restorative sleep, often seen as a metaphor for the ultimate rest in the afterlife.

The meticulous structure of the Hours does more than just anchor the monastic community in a daily rhythm; it serves as a constant reminder of their commitment to a higher spiritual calling. In an age where the ordinary and the sacred were often inseparable, Benedictine monks lived out a profound truth: every breath, every moment, was another opportunity for divine communion. These practices cultivate a continual state of vigilance and humility, echoing Benedict's call to "listen with the ear of your heart."

The interruptions caused by these daily offices bring a sense of order and transcendence to monastic life, bridging heaven and earth in a seamless continuum. By punctuating their day with these sacred pauses, monks internalize a rhythm that mirrors the natural cycles of life. In doing so, they do not withdraw from the world but rather immerse themselves in it more deeply, seeking the divine in every act, every thought, and every moment of stillness.

Seen through a broader lens, the Hours and Daily Offices speak to the utopian ideal embedded within Benedictine spirituality—a life in perfect harmony with divine will. Yet, this ideal also flirts with dystopian undertones, revealing human limitations, the struggle for consistency, and the ever-looming shadow of imperfection. Just as dawn breaks and twilight descends, the monastic life swings perpetually between aspiration and reality, sin and redemption.

By adhering to the structured ebb and flow of these sacred observances, Benedictines weave an intricate, living tapestry that narrates their unwavering devotion and ceaseless quest for divine intimacy. The Hours thus stand as timeless sentinels, guiding each monk through the labyrinth of their spiritual journey, illuminating pathways that lead not away from the world, but deeper into its heart, where the sacred and the mundane coalesce in a symphony of perpetual praise.

Chapter 7: Work and Community Life

In the intricate tapestry of Benedictine life, work and community intertwine as a singular thread, embodying a sacred rhythm that shapes the existence of its adherents. Labor, whether in the agricultural fields or within the monastery walls, transcends mere physical effort, emerging as a profound spiritual discipline. Saint Benedict's vision articulated labor as "prayer in action," thus infusing every task with divine purpose. Community life thrived through a symbiotic relationship, where each member's toil supported the collective's spiritual and material needs. Meanwhile, artisanal and scholarly endeavors enriched both the mind and soul, fostering a culture of continuous learning and perfection. This unity of work and community not only mirrored celestial harmony but also cultivated a haven of spiritual and practical sustenance, echoing the utopian ideals envisaged by Benedict and exemplified through the devotion and companionship of his sister, Scholastica. In this harmonious microcosm, the monastery demonstrated how labor, suffused with spiritual intent, could rebuild and sustain a holistic and devout human society on earth.

The Role of Labor in Monastic Life

In the grand tapestry of Benedictine existence, labor was more than mere toil; it was an intricate thread woven with spiritual and communal purpose. The Rule of Saint Benedict, with its foundational precept of "ora et labora" (pray and work), encapsulated a vision where manual and intellectual labor were pathways to divine unity and communal harmony. Through agricultural endeavors, monks engaged directly with the land, seeing in the cycles of sowing and harvest a reflection of divine providence and the rhythms of spiritual growth. Artisanal tasks and scholarly pursuits further expanded this ethos, transforming monasteries into beacons of cultural and intellectual preservation. The act of working together under a common purpose created an interdependence, where the humility of service and the dignity of work braided into a life of profound spiritual and communal richness. Thus, labor in monastic life was not just about sustaining the body, but nourishing the soul and fortifying the bonds of community.

Agricultural and Manual Work within the monastic domain holds a profound significance, echoing both practical necessity and theological virtue. Saint Benedict, in crafting his monastic rule, emphasized the harmonious balance between the spiritual and the physical, mirroring the divine equilibrium in creation. This focus on labor was not merely about sustenance but was imbued with deeper spiritual imperatives. The monks' engagement in agricultural work wasn't just a means to an end; it was an expression of their devotion and a critical part of their spiritual discipline.

In the early days at the monastery of Monte Cassino, the Benedictine monks faced the daunting task of transforming rugged, uncultivated land into fertile agricultural space. This arduous work demanded both physical endurance and ingenuity. They removed stones, tilled the earth, planted crops, and tended to livestock. Such tasks, though strenuous, were seen as expressions of obedience and humility. The very act of working the land became an allegory for the monks' inner cultivation of virtue and grace under God's gaze.

The rhythm of agricultural work was closely tied to the liturgical calendar. The seasons of planting and harvest paralleled the cycles of fasting and feasting, death and resurrection. Manual labor was, in many ways, a form of prayer—a means to align the physical with the divine. Benedict's Rule famously enjoined, "Ora et Labora," or "Pray and Work," blending sacred contemplation with the sanctification of daily toil. This union of labor and prayer exemplified a utopian vision where work is transformed from a burden into a holy and redemptive act.

The monastery itself became a microcosm of Eden, where the monks emulated the primordial harmony between humanity and nature. Agricultural and manual work, under Benedict's rule, was a return to the innocence of paradise—a striving to repair the fractured relationship between mankind and creation. In their gardens and fields, the monks cultivated not just plants but virtues, nurturing patience, diligence, and a spirit of community.

The products of the monks' labor served both practical and charitable purposes. The fruits, vegetables, and grains harvested were used to sustain the monastic community, providing nourishment essential for their lives of devotion and study. However, the surplus often found its way to the poor and needy, reflecting the Benedictine commitment to charity and hospitality. In this way, agricultural work became a channel for the monks to serve Christ in the least of their brethren, extending the monastic enclosure's sanctifying presence into the wider community.

This dual focus—on the interior cultivation of virtue and the exterior act of charity—illustrates the Benedictine vision of work as holistic. Agricultural labor was not merely functional but a form of communal prayer and an offering to God. By tending to the earth and caring for the least among them, the monks embodied a profound synthesis of faith and works, a living testimony to the Incarnational theology that underpins Christian doctrine.

Agricultural work also fostered a sense of unity and equality within the monastic community. Benedict's Rule insisted that all monks, regardless of their background or status, partake in manual labor. This dissolution of social hierarchies within the abbey echoed the early Christian ideal of communal living witnessed in the Acts of the Apostles. By working side by side in the fields, the monks cultivated not just crops, but brotherhood. The ethos of shared labor reinforced the Benedictine understanding of each monk's intrinsic value and the communal pursuit of holiness.

Beyond the fields, the Rule of Saint Benedict mandates a range of manual tasks, from cooking and cleaning to crafting and building. These tasks were integrated into the daily schedule, balancing toil with rest and prayer. Each monk, through his assigned duties, contributed to the well-being and maintenance of the monastery, underscoring the communal nature of their vocation. This structured approach to labor reflected Benedict's wisdom in fostering order, stability, and mutual support.

In this carefully choreographed symphony of work and worship, the monastery's physical and spiritual structures were firmly intertwined. The buildings and grounds, meticulously maintained by the monks, stood as tangible representations of their inner lives. Each stone laid, each plant nurtured, each task performed with diligence spoke to a deeper metaphysical order. The monastery was a fortress of faith, its well-tended garden a symbol of the soul's cultivation.

Thus, agricultural and manual work within Benedictine monasticism transcends mere survival. It is imbued with theological significance, rooted in a deep understanding of humanity's role in God's creation. Through their labor, the monks at Monte Cassino and other Benedictine monasteries forged a sacred bond with the earth, transforming the mundane into the divine, and labor into a liturgy of life.

Artisanal and Scholarly Work within the Benedictine monastic tradition reveals the profound depth of human creativity and intellectual pursuit—a harmonious blend of manual craftsmanship and scholarly diligence. The monks saw these activities as more than mere tasks; they were an extension of their spiritual endeavor and a path to divine contemplation. Their contributions during the medieval period not only shaped monastic life but also significantly impacted broader Western culture and intellectual heritage.

Artisanal work in Benedictine monasteries included a variety of crafts such as weaving, metalwork, woodcarving, and even brewing. Each monk contributed according to his God-given talents, believing that labor was sanctifying—an act inseparable from prayer. The fruits of their labor were often sold or traded, providing sustenance for the community and allowing the monks to carry out their spiritual and charitable missions without undue reliance on external benefactors.

This synthesis of labor and contemplation finds its roots in the Rule of Saint Benedict, which emphasizes the dignity of work and its role in shaping the human soul. Artisanal tasks were performed in a rhythm that mirrored the balance of prayer and study. Each monk, through dexterous hands and contemplative mind, contributed to the creation of objects that were both functional and beautiful, thus elevating the mundane to the realm of the sacred.

Of particular note is the Benedictine commitment to the scholarly work of copying manuscripts. Established scriptoria within monasteries became centers of intellectual preservation and dissemination. The painstaking process of manuscript illumination and copying was seen as an act of devotion. Through their meticulous work, monks preserved the wisdom of ancient texts—both sacred and secular—ensuring that the intellectual heritage of previous generations was passed down through the ages.

The scriptoria were bustling hubs of activity, where the sounds of quills scratching on parchment were constant. Here, monks labored to copy not only religious texts like the Bible, but also classical works of philosophy, science, and literature. This act of preservation was not a mere replication of words, but a form of worship. In copying texts, the monks led lives of profound humility and patience, qualities extolled by the Rule of Saint Benedict.

The scholarly output of the Benedictine monks extended beyond mere replication of texts. They contributed to original scholarship in theology, philosophy, and natural sciences. Their annotations and commentaries on various works added a new layer of understanding and set the stage for future scholarly pursuits. Monastic libraries became treasure troves of knowledge, accessible to the monks and, in some cases, to the broader scholarly community.

The interplay between artisanal and scholarly work in Benedictine monasteries exemplified a holistic approach to life—a life where the manual and intellectual labors were not in opposition, but in complementary harmony. The Rule of Saint Benedict enshrined the principle of "Ora et Labora" (Pray and Work), ensuring that monks engaged fully with the world around them while striving for spiritual transcendence.

The monks' approach to artisanal work also had profound social implications. Their products often found their way into local markets, influencing regional economies. By perfecting crafts and developing techniques that were later adopted by lay craftsmen, Benedictine monasteries became centers of technological and economic development. They fostered a culture of quality and devotion to excellence, principles that echoed beyond the cloister walls.

In the realm of scholarly work, the impact was equally far-reaching. The preservation and extension of knowledge by Benedictine monks helped to lay the foundations of Western education. Their scriptoria were the progenitors of later medieval universities, establishing a lineage that valued critical thinking and intellectual rigor. The carefully curated libraries of the monasteries became the repositories of collective wisdom, open to future generations of scholars who would build upon the intellectual heritage preserved by these diligent monks.

Thus, Benedictine monasteries served as beacons of light during times of intellectual darkness. In an era when invasions and upheavals threatened the stability of European civilization, these sanctuaries of learning kept the flame of knowledge alive. They provided a continuity of culture and thought, acting as custodians of tradition while also engaging with contemporary intellectual challenges.

Moreover, the artistic endeavors within monasteries were not limited to practical crafts or manuscripts. The creation of religious art such as illuminated manuscripts, sacred vestments, and ecclesiastical vessels was an integral part of monastic life. These works of art were not just expressions of aesthetic sensibility; they were visual theology—symbols and icons that communicated profound spiritual truths.

Certainly, the illuminated manuscripts deserve special mention. These manuscripts were not just books but were transformed into stunning works of art through intricate designs, vibrant colors, and intricate gold leaf decorations. Each stroke of the pen and brush was a deliberate act of devotion, capturing the beauty of the divine as perceived by the artist-monk. These sacred texts became mediums through which both the creators and the viewers could experience a deeper communion with the divine.

More than mere illustrations, these visual elements served as instructional tools for the faithful. In a time when literacy was not widespread, the artistry in these manuscripts made the Scriptures and theological concepts accessible to the broader populace, thus serving both an educational and a devotional purpose. Each piece was imbued with layers of meaning, intended to elevate the mind towards contemplation of divine mysteries.

Artisanal and scholarly activities within Benedictine monasteries were, therefore, more than practical necessities or academic exercises. They were expressions of a deeper spiritual journey—a journey that sought to unite the material and the spiritual, the temporal and the eternal. By immersing themselves in constant prayer and diligent labor, the monks transformed every aspect of their work into an act of worship, binding themselves to a rhythm that echoed the divine order.

In modern times, the legacy of Benedictine artisanal and scholarly work continues to inspire. Contemporary monastic communities still engage in crafts and scholarship, though the nature of these activities has evolved. In a world increasingly dominated by digital technology and hurried lifestyles, the Benedictine commitment to careful, deliberate work stands as a counter-cultural witness to the value of patience, focus, and dedication to excellence.

The time-tested tradition of blending manual and intellectual labor shows that true creativity and discovery are not confined to any one mode of work but flourish in the interplay between practical and theoretical pursuits. Monastic artisans and scholars cultivated an environment where labor was sanctified, knowledge was cherished, and every act was an opportunity to encounter the sacred. Their enduring influence reminds us that the pursuit of beauty and truth is a multifaceted endeavor, deeply embedded in the fabric of human existence.

One can conclude that the legacy of artisanal and scholarly work in Benedictine monasteries is a testament to the profound impact a life dedicated to "Ora et Labora" can have on individuals and society as a whole. By harmonizing work and contemplation, the monks created a living tradition that nurtures both the hands and the mind, fostering an environment where each person's unique gifts can flourish for the greater glory of God and the enrichment of human culture.

Chapter 8: Education and Preservation of Knowledge

Positioned at the intersection of spirituality and scholarship, the Benedictine commitment to education and the preservation of knowledge created an enduring legacy. Echoing through the dimly lit halls of monastic schools and the whisperings of the scriptoria, the labors of Benedictine monks were nothing short of monumental. By establishing structured environments where young minds could be nourished, monastic schools became the crucibles of Christian education, underscoring the importance of both divine and earthly wisdom. Parallel to this, the scriptoria stood as the silent guardians of human heritage, with meticulous copying of manuscripts ensuring the survival of classical texts and sacred scriptures. These twin pillars of education and preservation were not just acts of devotion but also subtle acts of rebellion against the encroaching oblivion of the Dark Ages. Thus, Benedict and Scholastica's collective vision—rooted in a utopian synthesis of labor, prayer, and study—paved the way for a succession of enlightened generations, safeguarding the flame of knowledge against the tempests of time.

Monastic Schools and Scriptoria

The heart and soul of Benedictine monasticism lay in its scriptoria and monastic schools, where an intricate dance between divine contemplation and scholastic endeavor flourished. These sanctuaries of knowledge transcended mere education; they were utopias of intellect and spirit, breathing life into worn parchments and sacred texts. Monks, in a disciplined symphony of labor and devotion, meticulously copied manuscripts, ensuring the preservation of theological, philosophical, and classical works. The schools, nurturing minds in this sanctified atmosphere, became beacons of erudition in a world often shrouded in ignorance. Here, under the watchful eyes of St. Benedict and St. Scholastica's spiritual legacy, the pursuit of knowledge intertwined beautifully with the quest for divine truth, fostering an unbroken chain of wisdom through the ages.

Copying and Preserving Manuscripts ... within the solemn walls of Benedictine monasteries, scribes embarked upon a mission that was as spiritual as it was scholarly. Copying and preserving manuscripts wasn't just a job, it was viewed as a sacred duty, one that connected the monks not only to their faith but also to the future of human knowledge.

In the stark quietness of the scriptorium, the room designated for this purpose, monks often worked alone, illuminated by the soft glow of candles. The meticulous task of copying texts required immense discipline and patience, virtues that were cultivated in the daily life of the monastery. Each letter, each word painstakingly transcribed, became a testament to both human dedication and divine inspiration. These rooms were not simply workplaces; they were sanctuaries of thought where the sacred and the scholarly merged seamlessly. Monks saw themselves as guardians, preserving the wisdom of the ages for future generations.

It's important to understand that these manuscripts weren't just copies of religious texts, though Scriptures and liturgical books were paramount. The scribes also transcribed works of philosophy, medicine, and science. In doing so, they became bridges between antiquity and the medieval world, ensuring that the intellectual heritage of early Christians, Greeks, and Romans was not lost to time. The diversity of the manuscripts was a testament to the Benedictine commitment to both spiritual and intellectual growth.

Among the most revered items in a scriptorium were the codices containing the Scriptures. Monks treated these texts with the utmost reverence, often marking them with elaborate illuminations and gold leaf. These embellishments were not merely decorative but were visual meditations that invited contemplation. In a sense, the monks were not just copying texts; they were worshipping through their craft, imbuing each page with a sense of the holy.

The process of copying and preserving manuscripts was highly formalized, governed by rules that ensured the accuracy and quality of the texts. Each manuscript would begin with the careful preparation of the vellum or parchment. This was no small task; it required months of preparation to ensure that the writing surface was perfectly smooth and free from imperfections. The selection of inks and pigments further showcased the monks' dedication to their craft, with some even traveling great distances to procure the finest materials.

Once the materials were prepared, the act of writing could begin. Monks would often work from a master copy, carefully comparing their work line by line to avoid mistakes. Errors were corrected immediately, and some scribes developed personalized symbols and shorthand methods to enhance their efficiency and accuracy. Marginal notes and glosses would sometimes accompany the main text, providing commentary or clarification. In this way, manuscripts became living documents, enriched by the insights and wisdom of generations of monks.

Moreover, the Benedictines understood the importance of teaching and knowledge transmission. Monasteries housed schools where new generations of monks and sometimes even laypeople could learn the skills of reading, writing, and copying. This educational focus ensured that the sacred duty of manuscript preservation would continue unabated, passing from one generation to the next. The monastic school was thus an incubator of literacy and learning, perpetuating a cycle of educational and spiritual enrichment.

Benedictine hospitality extended even to the intellectual domain. Scholars from various parts of the world would come to these monastic centers to study and make copies of manuscripts. In this way, monasteries became hubs of learning and scholarship, spreading knowledge far beyond their walls. It was a form of intellectual outreach that paid rich dividends, contributing greatly to the cultural and intellectual vibrancy of medieval Europe.

Of course, the work of preserving manuscripts wasn't solely about the preservation of text. There was also a keen awareness of the time's political and social upheavals. Wars, invasions, and natural disasters posed constant threats to these invaluable collections. Many monks heroically risked their lives to safeguard these manuscripts, hiding them in secret compartments within monastery walls or transporting them across treacherous terrains to safer locations. In some cases, entire libraries were relocated to ensure their survival, reflecting the monks' deep commitment to their mission.

This devotion to preservation was amplified by the Benedictine vow of stability, which anchored monks to their communities for life. The stability of the monastic community stood as a bulwark against the chaos of the outside world, and it was within this stable environment that manuscripts could be safely copied, studied, and stored. The monastery was a world unto itself, one where the rhythms of daily life provided a structured, serene backdrop for intellectual endeavors.

It should also be noted that these activities weren't without their moments of spiritual and philosophical reflection. The arduous task of manuscript preservation was often accompanied by a meditative contemplation of the texts themselves. As the ink flowed from their quills, monks pondered the eternal truths contained within the writings. This reflective practice enriched their spiritual lives and deepened their connection to the divine.

In a sense, the scriptorium was a crucible where the spiritual and intellectual formed a harmonious dialectic. The act of copying manuscripts required not only technical skill but also a profound sense of purpose. Each stroke of the quill was a devotional act, an offering to God and a pledge to future generations. Within these hallowed halls, the interplay of shadows and light reflected the eternal struggle between ignorance and knowledge, chaos and order.

The legacy of these monastic endeavors is monumental, with countless manuscripts surviving to this day as witnesses to this Benedictine dedication. Their contributions laid the foundation for the Renaissance, enabling a rediscovery of classical texts and the flowering of humanism. The humble scribes, toiling in the silence of their scriptoria, thus became pivotal figures in the grand narrative of Western civilization. Their work ensured the continuity of culture, the preservation of wisdom, and the illumination of minds across the millennia.

Ultimately, the act of copying and preserving manuscripts within Benedictine monasticism transcended mere academic duty. It was a sacred trust, a melding of vocation and devotion that echoed the divine call to steward creation and safeguard the treasures of human knowledge. This painstaking labor of love stands as a timeless testament to the enduring power of faith and intellect united in purpose.

Chapter 9: Benedictine Monks in Society

Benedictine monks, with their rhythmic cycles of prayer, labor, and study, profoundly shaped the societies they inhabited. When the outside world battled chaos, these monks sparked order, uniting spirituality with physical toil. Their tireless outreach extended not only to the poor and sick, providing care that went beyond mere almsgiving, but also to the local communities, creating ripples of influence that underscored the interconnectedness of all lives. Their monasteries became bastions of stability, centers of education, and bulwarks of charity, reflecting a utopian vision where divine grace met human resilience. Here, the silent whisper of their disciplined existence spoke volumes, integrating Heaven's ideals with Earth's realities, and charting a course for harmonious living that society could follow. Through the embodiment of their principles, Benedictine monks became both the heartbeat and the balm of the medieval world, continuously molding and nurturing the civic fabric around them.

Outreach and Charity

In a world cloistered by walls of both stone and spirit, the Benedictine monks carried the light of mercy and grace beyond their sacred confines through outreach and charity. This was not a mere act of duty, but rather an expression of their profound belief in the interconnectedness of all humanity. Rooted in the Rule of Saint Benedict, which emphasizes the sanctity of hospitality, these monks extended their compassion to the poor, the sick, and the needy. Their monasteries became sanctuaries, offering both spiritual solace and material aid, thereby transforming desolate hearts and barren lands alike. Through their charitable works, they manifested an ideal society where love and care for one another were not utopian dreams but daily practices. This equilibrium of prayer and action illuminated a path for others to follow, creating ripples of benevolence that extended far beyond the monastery walls and touched the very fabric of medieval society.

Care for the Poor and Sick has always been a cornerstone of Benedictine monasticism, an embodiment of the community's devotion to living out the tenets of Christian charity. Saint Benedict's Rule explicitly mandates hospitality and care for those in need, emphasizing the monks' role as servants to the poor and infirm. Rooted in the teachings of Christ, Benedict's instructions highlight the imperative to see Christ in every guest, particularly the marginalized and suffering.

It was at Monte Cassino where these principles first took tangible form. Saint Benedict established a practice whereby the poor received food, shelter, and medical care. The monastery became a sanctuary, a place of refuge where the walls seemed to breathe with the love and compassion of its inhabitants. Unlike the opulent and often detached charitable acts of the wealthy, Benedictine care was integrated into daily life. The monks engaged with those they helped, creating a bond of mutual respect and spiritual kinship.

The Rule of Saint Benedict profoundly shaped this ideal. "Let all guests who arrive be received like Christ," Benedict wrote, instituting a practice that extended to the sick and poor. These words were not a mere formality; they demanded a deeply personal and active love. Visitors to the monastery could testify to the genuine care and concern they received. It was this living out of Christ's commandment to love one's neighbor that set the Benedictine approach apart from other charitable models of the time.

Saint Scholastica, no less devoted than her brother, contributed to this emphasis on charity. While the historical records about her life are less detailed, her reputed acts of kindness and hospitality underscore the shared values. Scholastica's convent reflected the same principles, serving as a place where the poor and sick could find solace and support. The twin pillars of Benedictine monasticism thus stood united in their mission to turn compassion into action.

In the medieval world, health care was primitive and often inaccessible to the lower classes. Monasteries filled this void, providing care that the state could not. They housed infirmaries staffed by monks who were both caregivers and spiritual guides. Herbs from meticulously maintained gardens served as medicine, and holistic approaches to health blended spiritual and physical care. This not only healed bodies but also restored spirits, offering a rare source of integral well-being in those times.

The emphasis on caring for the poor and sick is not just an historical footnote but a prophetic vision. By intertwining charity with everyday monastic life, Saint Benedict and Saint Scholastica showcased a utopian vision of society. Their approach illustrated how communities based on mutual support and genuine care could thrive against the backdrop of a world often marked by social inequity and neglect. They demonstrated that true strength lies not in dominion but in service, not in accumulation but in giving.

Imagine a world where each community took it upon itself to care for its most vulnerable members. The Benedictine model suggests a society healed by the bonds of compassion rather than one fractured by indifference. Utopian in its simplicity, this approach calls for a reconsideration of what it means to lead a fulfilling life. Indeed, the care for the poor and sick as observed by the Benedictines stands as an allegory for the transformative power of love and compassion.

This commitment to charity was not without its challenges. The monasteries often stretched their limited resources to the brink, compelled by their unwavering mission of service. Yet, this strain highlighted the profound faith and dedication of the monastic communities. Their works were acts of resistance against a world more inclined to overlook the needy. In caring for the weakest members of society, the Benedictines strengthened the very fabric of the community, ensuring that no one was left behind.

From a philosophical standpoint, this Benedictine ethos of care serves as a dialogue between the temporal and the eternal. It proclaims that spiritual growth is inextricably linked to acts of mercy and love. The monks and nuns, in their humble service, continually engaged in a form of living theology. Their daily actions preached sermons that words alone could not convey, making their entire lives a testament to their beliefs.

The physical structures of monasteries themselves often reflected this commitment. Infirmaries and guesthouses were not tucked away but integrated into the very heart of monastic life. This architectural choice symbolized the central role of charity in Benedictine spirituality. The layout suggested a community where barriers between the healthy and sick, the rich and poor, were deliberately blurred.

The influence of Benedictine care extended far beyond the walls of the monasteries. Local communities, observing the monks' model, were inspired to adopt similar practices. Villages near these monastic centers often saw improvements in the welfare of their populations, as the monasteries' acts of charity became communal norms. Thus, the Benedictine influence rippled outward, affecting broader societal patterns.

Even in modern contexts, the legacy of this caring spirit can be felt. Contemporary Benedictine institutions, though worlds apart from their medieval foundations, continue to prioritize outreach and social justice. Their hospitals, clinics, and charitable organizations embody the same principles laid out by Saint Benedict and Scholastica, proving that their foresight and compassion are timeless.

The future of this mission lies in its ability to adapt while staying true to its foundational principles. As new challenges arise, the enduring values of care and compassion will undoubtedly guide Benedictine communities in their responses. The Rule of Saint Benedict remains a living document, ready to inspire new generations to see the face of Christ in every person, especially the poor and the sick.

In summation, the Benedictine care for the poor and sick reflects a comprehensive approach to Christian charity. It intertwines spiritual and physical healing, offering a holistic model of care that remains relevant. From its early roots in the monasteries of Saint Benedict and Saint Scholastica to its modern adaptations, this mission continues to shine as a beacon of compassion and service. In their quiet, consistent acts of mercy, the

Benedictines exemplify a utopian vision grounded in lived reality, urging us all to see and serve Christ in our neighbors.

Influence on Local Communities

The Benedictine monastic tradition, established by Saints Benedict and Scholastica, fundamentally shaped the character and dynamics of the local communities where these monasteries were founded. One cannot fully grasp the historical and cultural landscapes of medieval Europe without acknowledging the profound and multilayered impact of these religious communities. Through their daily interactions, charitable deeds, and the embodying of their spiritual precepts, the Benedictine monks and nuns became integral to the very fabric of local life and society.

Within these communities, the monasteries served as beacons of stability and centers of learning, especially during periods of political turmoil and social upheaval. The Rule of Saint Benedict, with its emphasis on prayer, work, and study, provided a structured rhythm to life that extended beyond the confines of the monastery. Monks and nuns often engaged in agricultural activities, scholarly pursuits, and artisanal crafts, thereby not only sustaining themselves but also contributing to the economic vitality of the surrounding regions.

Considering the agricultural prowess of the Benedictine order, their knowledge in land management and agricultural techniques was disseminated to the local peasantry, elevating farming practices and productivity. The cultivation of herbs, fruits, and vegetables, as well as the maintenance of vineyards and livestock, were areas where the monks demonstrated exceptional expertise. By sharing their agricultural know-how, they helped improve local food supplies and fostered a sense of communal well-being and resilience.

Moreover, Benedictine monasteries were epicenters of artisanal craftsmanship. The monks were known for producing high-quality goods—ranging from textiles to religious artifacts—that were placed in local markets. These crafted items were not just commodities; they were embodiments of the spiritual discipline and devotion poured into their creation. This seamless integration of material and spiritual life left an indelible mark on the local economies and cultural landscapes.

Education was another significant arena where the Benedictine influence was felt deeply. Monasteries often housed schools where local children could receive instruction in reading, writing, and religious studies. In a time when educational opportunities were limited, these monastic schools offered essential gateways to knowledge and personal development. The pedagogical contributions of the Benedictine order thus had a long-lasting impact, cultivating generations of educated individuals who would go on to serve various roles in broader society.

Charity and hospitality were central pillars of Benedictine life, grounded in the teachings of Saint Benedict himself. Monasteries provided refuge and aid to the poor, the sick, and travelers. In this sense, the Benedictine institutions functioned as proto-social service organizations, long before the advent of modern welfare states. Their practice of welcoming strangers and assisting those in need reinforced communal bonds and fostered an ethos of compassion and mutual support.

The spiritual guidance offered by Benedictine monks and nuns extended well beyond the cloister walls. Through sermons, confessions, and spiritual counseling, they addressed the moral and existential concerns of their communities. Often acting as intermediaries between the divine and the secular, they provided a moral compass that helped shape community norms and values. Their influence was not merely doctrinal but penetrated the everyday lives of the people.

It's also essential to consider the role of the Benedictine liturgy in bringing the community together. The rhythm of daily prayers and the celebration of the Eucharist created a spiritual ecosystem that provided a sense of continuity and belonging. Local people were often invited to participate in monastic liturgies, thus intertwining the spiritual lives of the monks with those of the lay community. The experience of shared worship fostered a collective spiritual identity, knitting the social fabric tighter.

The libraries and scriptoria within Benedictine monasteries were fonts of intellectual activity and preservation. By copying and preserving manuscripts, the monks became the custodians of knowledge, ensuring the transmission of classical texts and religious works through generations. This intellectual labor was not an isolated endeavor but one that buttressed the cultural heritage of their localities and, by extension, the broader Christian world.

While the boundaries of the monastery were clearly defined, the influence of the Benedictine monks permeated every aspect of local life. Their presence offered a stabilizing force and a source of moral and spiritual guidance. The dual commitment to contemplative life and active engagement in labor and education created a symbiotic relationship with the surrounding communities, one that brought temporal and spiritual benefits alike.

To distill the essence of the Benedictine impact on local communities is to recognize that they were both catalysts of change and anchors of stability. In their commitment to the Rule of Saint Benedict, they didn't merely pursue personal salvation but envisioned and enacted a microcosm of an ideal society where work, prayer, and communal well-being were seamlessly integrated. The magnetic influence they exerted extended outward, drawing individuals and families into a shared vision of a life well-lived, where the temporal and eternal realms coexisted harmoniously.

As we reflect upon this enduring legacy, it becomes clear that the Benedictine monks and nuns embodied a utopian ideal that mirrored the highest aspirations of their faith yet found pragmatic expression in their daily interactions with local communities. Their lives of disciplined devotion, service, and scholarship created ripples that would reverberate through history, offering a testament to the enduring power of faith in shaping the human world.

Chapter 10: Medieval Spread of Benedictine Practices

The medieval period heralded an extraordinary diffusion of Benedictine practices across Europe, shaping the spiritual landscape in ways both profound and enduring. The establishment of new monasteries became a beacon of order amid the chaos of feudal fragmentation, each one a citadel of prayer, work, and community life. These monasteries spread like seeds in fertile soil, bringing with them the transformative Rule of Saint Benedict which emphasized balance, humility, and communal living. Envisioned as utopian enclaves in a dystopian world, these monastic communities cultivated a unique culture that knit together diverse social fabrics, promoting both individual and collective sanctity. The practices codified by Saint Benedict and disseminated through monastic networks not only preserved sacred knowledge but also fostered agricultural innovation and artisanal craftsmanship. As these practices flourished, they became emblematic of a divine order that sought to transcend the temporal struggles of the era, calling all towards a higher unity and serene contemplation.

Expansion Across Europe

The medieval expansion of Benedictine practices across Europe is a tale woven from divine providence and the human striving for spiritual perfection. As the seeds of Saint Benedict's Rule were carried by peregrinating monks, they found fertile soil in a myriad of cultural and geographic landscapes. From the rugged highlands of Scotland to the sun-soaked plains of Spain, monasteries sprouted like ecclesiastical beacons, guiding souls toward contemplative labor and communal holiness. These monastic enclaves, far more than mere edifices of stone, became crucibles of learning and sanctity, influencing local customs, education, and even governance. The dissemination of Benedictine ideals crafted not just spiritual havens but also fortified networks of social stability and intellectual vigor, transforming Europe into a mosaic of devout and industrious communities, each echoing the disciplined, yet profoundly humane teachings of Saints Benedict and Scholastica.

Establishment of New Monasteries The medieval spread of Benedictine practices wasn't solely a tale of mere geographic expansion; it was a spiritual journey, a quest for divine perfection and communal sanctity. Where Dark Ages cloaked Europe in unsettling uncertainties, the monasteries stood as beacons of light, sanctuaries of stability and learning. Saint Benedict of Nursia's Rule, imbued with wisdom and foresight, acted as the anchor for these nascent communities. Each new establishment was more than a building; it was the embodiment of a living tradition, a tangible manifestation of divine grace and human diligence.

These early monasteries sprouted from the intentions and spiritual aspirations of their founders, often shaped by the unique needs and circumstances of each locality. Europe in the Middle Ages was a fragmented land of diverse cultures and traditions, yet, paradoxically, the Rule of Saint Benedict transcended these barriers, offering a universal blueprint for monastic life. It's worth pondering how Benedict's ethos, so meticulously designed, could adapt to such varied contexts. Perhaps, it was the Rule's inherent flexibility and deep understanding of human nature that allowed it to flourish in disparate conditions.

The process of founding a new monastery typically began with a small group of monks, sometimes dispatched from an established abbey, other times inspired by a spiritual calling. These foundational monks bore the heavy responsibility of not only erecting physical structures but also cultivating the spiritual essence of their new community. While buildings could be raised with stone and timber, the inner strength of a monastery was often found in its adherence to the principles of the Rule. This endeavor required a harmonious blend of contemplation and action, of ora et labora—prayer and work.

Such establishments were often initialized by local nobles or bishops, who recognized the civilizing influence that a monastery could exert on a region. These patrons provided the essential land and resources, hoping that the monastic presence would bring not only spiritual benefits but also educational and economic revitalization. In return, the monks offered prayers for the souls of their benefactors, weaving a complex web of spiritual and temporal relationships. This symbiotic relationship was just as pragmatic as it was pious— an interplay of grace and survival.

Consider Monte Cassino, founded by Saint Benedict himself. Nestled atop a rugged hill, it serves as the archetype of monastic resilience and spiritual fortitude. Despite the initial hardships—including raids and natural disasters—the community endured, its endurance a testament to the eternal words inscribed in Benedict's Rule. Each new monastery endeavored to replicate this model of tenacity and spiritual focus, creating a network of interconnected communities, each a bulwark against the chaos of the age.

Equally important was the careful selection of leadership. Abbots were chosen with great caution, as these individuals would bear the ultimate responsibility for the spiritual and administrative well-being of the new community. The Abbot was both a spiritual father and a pragmatic steward, ensuring that the monastery adhered to the Rule while also meeting the physical needs of its inhabitants. This duality of roles called for a delicate balance, a reality that every founding community faced with solemnity and earnest prayer.

Historians often marvel at the speed and efficiency with which these monasteries proliferated across Europe. Within a few centuries, Benedictine monasteries dotted the landscape from the Iberian Peninsula to the British Isles, from the plains of France to the rolling hills of Italy and beyond. This rapid expansion was not merely a result of strategic planning but an organic outgrowth of the profound spiritual hunger that pervaded the continent. Monks became the torchbearers of this spiritual renaissance, crossing mountains and rivers, enduring hardships, driven by an unwavering commitment to their monastic calling.

It's fascinating to delve into why these monasteries became so successful. A critical factor was their self-sufficiency. The Rule of Saint Benedict emphasized the importance of labor, not merely as a practical necessity, but as a spiritual exercise. Each monastery became an epicenter of agricultural and artisanal activity, fostering a microcosm of sustainable living. This work was not just outwardly productive; it was a form of service to God, an act of divine worship through the labor of hands and the sweat of the brow.

The new monasteries served as oases of stability in a world frequently marred by war, famine, and social upheaval. The Benedictine commitment to education and manuscript preservation further amplified their influence. Monastic scriptoria became bustling centers of intellectual activity, copying and preserving ancient texts that might otherwise have been lost to history. In these quiet halls, the wisdom of antiquity found refuge, its secrets inscribed by diligent monks who viewed each manuscript as a vessel of divine truth.

This intellectual labor extended beyond mere preservation. Monastic schools emerged as centers of learning, offering instruction not only in religious matters but also in arts and sciences. These educational endeavors allowed monasteries to cultivate a continuous flow of literate and capable individuals who would go on to impact broader secular and ecclesiastical realms. The monasteries thus became crucibles of knowledge, their libraries miniature arks safeguarding the heritage of Western civilization.

The community life established in these new monasteries also presented a unique social paradigm. Here, in the cloistered confines, monks lived not as isolated ascetics but as members of a spiritual family, bound together by the Rule and their common love for Christ. This form of communal life was a radical counterpoint to the fragmented and often chaotic existence outside the monastery walls. Within, they found unity and purpose, a collective striving towards divine perfection.

It's important to note the role of women in this monastic movement as well. Convents were essential aspects of Benedictine expansion, guided by the principles laid down by Saint Scholastica, Benedict's twin sister, and her spiritual heirs. These communities provided a haven for women to pursue religious vocations, mirroring their male counterparts in their devotion to prayer, work, and communal living. The dual growth of monasteries and convents underscored the Benedictine vision of a comprehensive, inclusive spiritual landscape.

As these various threads of monastic life wove together, they formed a rich tapestry, each new monastery adding a stitch in the grand design of Christian Europe. The Benedictine networks facilitated not only religious observance but also social cohesion, economic stability, and intellectual growth. Each new foundation stood as a testament to the enduring legacy of Saints Benedict and Scholastica, their vision perpetuated through the diligent, faithful work of countless monks and nuns.

In retrospect, the establishment of new monasteries was no less than a utopian pursuit within a dystopian world. These monastic enclaves, governed by the Rule's divine order, stood as microcosms of ideal Christian living, aiming to restore humanity's lost Eden within the bounds of cloistered walls. In doing so, they offered more than a refuge from the world; they proffered a vision of what the world might become if it heeded the eternal wisdom enshrined in the Benedictine way of life.

Chapter 11: Reform Movements Within Benedictinism

As the Benedictine tradition blossomed across Europe, it faced both the challenge and opportunity of reform. The Cluniac Reforms emerged as a significant movement aimed at revitalizing the monastic fervor that seemed to wane with the passage of centuries. Rooted in the conviction that a purer adherence to the Rule of Saint Benedict could restore sanctity and communal integrity, these reforms sought to disentangle monastic life from feudal entanglements and secular distractions. The Cluniac reforms underscored the importance of liturgical devotion and communal prayer, becoming a beacon of spiritual renewal. This wave of reform not only reinvigorated monastic practices but also forged a new path that resonated with the original vision of Saint Benedict. In doing so, it highlighted the enduring relevance of Benedictine principles, while opening a dialogue for future movements that would continue to shape the course of monastic history.

Cluniac Reforms

In the heart of the tumultuous medieval era, the Cluniac Reforms emerged as a beacon of renewal within Benedictine monasticism, resounding through the cloisters of Christendom like an echo from the original ascetic vision of Saint Benedict. These reforms, initiated at the Abbey of Cluny in the early 10th century, sought not merely a return to the austere discipline of the Rule, but a transcendental renaissance of spiritual fervor and communal purity. Fuelled by a potent combination of hierarchical independence and devout rigor, the movement rose against the laxity and secular entanglements that plagued many monasteries. It championed an ideal of monastic life that intertwined unceasing prayer, sacred liturgy, and a detachment from worldly influences, ultimately fostering a network of reformed priories united in a celestial harmony of purpose. The Cluniac Reforms underscored a utopian aspiration within the Benedictine tradition, emphasizing an unwavering devotion to God in the relentless pursuit of a sanctified kingdom on earth. Through Cluny's celestial melody, the echoes of Benedict's holy vision were amplified, reverberating throughout a Christendom yearning for spiritual and communal redemption.

Aims and Achievements cannot be discussed without acknowledging the transformative aspirations that fueled the Cluniac reforms within the grand tradition of Benedictinism. At the dawn of the 10th century, the world was no stranger to the tumultuous waves of change. Yet it was amidst this backdrop that the Cluniac reforms emerged with specific aims, standing resolute against the prevailing challenges of their time. These reforms sought to restore the spiritual vitality and moral integrity that they believed were eroding within the monastic communities.

The Cluniac movement set its sights on a lofty goal: the rejuvenation of monastic life, rooted deeply in the Benedictine ethos. This was not just about returning to the strict rules but about elevating the communal life through a renewed commitment to prayer, liturgy, and communal interdependence. This aspiration was manifested in their emphasis on the "ora et labora" principle—prayer and work. They believed that the pure, undistracted devotion to these core tenets would elevate the spiritual consciousness of the monks and, by extension, benefit the broader Christian community.

One of the monumental achievements of the Cluniac reforms was their meticulous structuring of liturgical practices. The reforms introduced a rigorous schedule of divine office that ensured the constant presence of prayer and worship throughout the day and night. By fostering an environment where spiritual exercises were intertwined with daily routines, the Cluniac houses became bastions of divine communion. This continuous cycle of worship not only reinforced a spiritual discipline among the monks but also elevated the sense of communal sanctity.

The Cluniac reforms also placed a heavy emphasis on the observance of silence within the monastery walls. They believed that through silence, monks could better attune themselves to the divine presence, fostering a deeper inner dialogue with God. The quietude was not simply an absence of noise but a space filled with the potential for spiritual reflection and growth. This austere practice of silence was both a path to personal sanctification and a collective aspiration towards a higher spiritual cadence.

In addition to their liturgical enhancements, the Cluniacs were dedicated to the principle of monastic autonomy. They aimed to safeguard their communities from the secular entanglements that often plagued monastic establishments. By advocating for independence from feudal lords and local diocesan interference, they sought to maintain the purity and integrity of monastic life. This autonomy allowed their abbots to focus inward, fostering an environment where spiritual development was the paramount objective.

The influence of the Cluniac reforms was not confined to spiritual practices alone; it extended to architectural achievements as well. The construction of the Cluny Abbey, which became the largest church in Christendom before Saint Peter's Basilica, stands as a testimony to their grandeur and ambition. This architectural marvel was more than a physical structure; it was a symbol of the divine aspirations that the Cluniacs held dear. The intricate designs and vast spaces were intended to elevate the mind and spirit towards the heavenly realm, fulfilling their aim of creating a 'heaven on earth.'

The Cluniacs also achieved significant advancements in the organization and administration of monastic life. By establishing a network of daughter houses that were directly dependent on the mother house at Cluny, they created a centralized structure that ensured uniformity and adherence to their rigorous standards. This network was held together by regular visits and communications, fostering a sense of unity and mutual support among the various monasteries. This centralized organization helped to maintain high standards of monastic discipline and spirituality across different regions.

The emphasis on education and intellectual achievement was another notable aim of the Cluniac reforms. They established scriptoria and libraries, where the copying and preservation of texts became a sacred duty. This endeavor was crucial in a time when the knowledge of antiquity was at risk of being lost. The scriptoria not only preserved spiritual and theological texts but also classical works of literature and science, making them invaluable custodians of cultural heritage.

The Cluniac reforms also aspired to aid the poor and care for the sick, reflecting their deep commitment to the Benedictine ethos of hospitality. By establishing hospitals and almonries, the Cluniac monasteries extended their influence beyond their walls, becoming centers of charity and compassion. This commitment to social responsibility demonstrated their holistic approach to monastic life, where spiritual aspirations were intertwined with acts of mercy towards the less fortunate.

However, the lofty aims of the Cluniac reforms were not without their challenges. The very success of these monasteries often attracted wealth and patronage, which ironically posed a threat to their foundational principles of simplicity and poverty. The influx of riches and endowments risked diverting the focus from spiritual aspiration to material accumulation, a paradox that the Cluniacs had to constantly navigate.

Despite these challenges, the achievements of the Cluniac reforms had a profound impact on the monastic landscape of medieval Europe. They inspired a wave of renewal across the continent, with many monastic communities adopting and adapting the Cluniac principles. This widespread influence underscored the success of their vision and their ability to address the spiritual and organizational needs of their time.

The Cluniac reforms stand as a testament to the enduring power of Benedictine spirituality when it is pursued with clarity of purpose and steadfast dedication. Their achievements were not just architectural or administrative; they were transformations of the soul and spirit, aiming to align the earthly life of monks with a divine ideal. The reforms exemplified the belief that through dedicated communal living, rigorous prayer, and disciplined work, the monastic community could become a mirror of the heavenly kingdom, reflecting its order, beauty, and sanctity.

In conclusion, the aims and achievements of the Cluniac reforms were deeply interwoven with their aspiration to restore and elevate the spiritual life of monastic communities. Through their innovations in liturgical practice, architectural grandeur, organizational structure, and social responsibility, they created a legacy that transcended their era. Their commitment to the principles of Saint Benedict and their ability to adapt these to meet the needs of their time ensured that the Cluniac reforms would leave an indelible mark on the history of monasticism and the broader Christian tradition.

Chapter 12: Influence of the Benedictine Tradition in Art and Architecture

The Benedictine tradition, grounded in the sturdy Rule of Saint Benedict, has left an indelible mark on art and architecture. Monastic communities, committed to ora et labora (prayer and work), channeled their devotion into the creation and preservation of sacred spaces. These sanctuaries, notably adorned with intricate iconography and rich symbolism, illuminate the spiritual fervor of the monks. Within the walls of monasteries and abbeys, grand yet humble designs reflect the divine order and contemplative life urged by Benedictine principles. Architectural elements such as the spacious cloisters and the meticulously planned chapter houses fostered communal unity and individual solitude. The harmonious balance in these structures parallels the Benedictine aim of blending physical labor with spiritual contemplation, embodying a utopian vision of celestial order in earthly realms. Through their architectural endeavors, the Benedictines not only crafted sanctuaries of peace but also left a lasting heritage that continues to inspire awe and reverence.

Monastic Church Design

Monastic church design, imbued with the serene and contemplative spirit of the Benedictine tradition, serves as a testament to the synthesis of divine purpose and human craftsmanship. Each architectural element within these sacred spaces - from the austere yet reverent lines of the nave to the harmonious proportions of the cloister - reflects the principles of the Rule of Saint Benedict. These structures are not merely buildings; they are physical manifestations of a spiritual journey, where the labyrinthine corridors echo the path of sanctity and discipline, and the soaring arches invite the soul to ascend toward the heavenly. The integration of natural light through strategically placed windows and the use of locally sourced materials emphasize a symbiotic relationship with creation, mirroring the Benedictine ethos of stability and respect for the environment. These churches stand as utopian embodiments of a community life entirely devoted to seeking divine wisdom and embodying the balance between ora et labora, prayer and work, guiding the faithful into deeper contemplation and unity.

Iconography and Symbolism serve as a cryptic language that unfolds the spiritual truths rooted in the lives of Saints Benedict and Scholastica. These visual elements not only represent their historical and spiritual significance but also evoke the contemplative ethos embodied by Benedictine monasticism.

The most prevalent symbol associated with Saint Benedict is often the crosier, an ecclesiastical staff indicative of his role as an abbot and shepherd of monastic life. This staff, curved at the top, symbolizes guiding leadership, reflecting both governance and pastoral care. Frequently depicted with an open book, Saint Benedict emphasizes the "Rule," a guiding manuscript on monastic living. The book signifies not just knowledge but divine order, harmonizing human endeavor with celestial wills.

Complementing these symbols is the raven, integral to Benedictine iconography. Tradition holds that a raven miraculously saved Saint Benedict from poisoned bread, symbolizing divine intervention and wisdom. The raven stands as a testament to spiritual vigilance against malevolent forces, that in the shadows of sin, divine providence watches over the faithful.

Turning to Saint Scholastica, her iconography is imbued with a sense of spiritual equality and unity with her brother Benedict. Often portrayed in simple monastic attire, she embodies humility and devotion. A notable symbol is the dove, which powerfully recalls the scene of her soul ascending to heaven. This imagery underscores the purity of her spiritual aspirations and the blessedness of her departure from earthly toil.

The intertwined stories of Benedict and Scholastica find expression in a unique set of symbols: the twin stars. These stars often depicted together illustrate a cosmic duality and harmony that echo their spiritual companionship. The stars also nod to the divine light each spread in their respective realms, acting as beacons of monastic wisdom and virtue.

Reflections of their lives extend into the architectural designs of monastic churches and abbeys. The labyrinth, frequently found in flooring designs, invites visitors into a meditative journey, echoing the disciplined path outlined in the "Rule of Saint Benedict." Walking these sacred spirals, one cannot help but ponder the interplay between life's complexities and divine simplicity. Such motifs deepen the allegorical landscape in which these saints' legacies are enshrined.

Sacred objects also carry rich symbolism. In particular, the chalice and host, used during the Eucharist, remind us of Saint Benedict's dedication to liturgical precision. The chalice symbolizes the sacred vessel of salvation, aligning with Benedict's vision of monastic life as both a container and conduit of divine grace. Every element in a liturgical setting, down to the smallest detail, resonates with the profound intentions set out by these holy figures.

Bells in Benedictine monasteries serve as another profound iconographic element. More than just instruments marking time, they signal the call to prayer and labor, echoing the balance of "ora et labora" central to Benedictine life. The resonant sound of a bell symbolizes the harmonious integration of the heavenly and earthly dimensions, a dual focus championed by both Saints Benedict and Scholastica.

When one casts an eye over illuminated manuscripts and stained glass windows, vivid depictions of these symbols leap to life. Here, artistry becomes exegesis, translating theological insights into visual narratives. Each stroke and color choice serves not merely as decoration but as a deliberate conduit of spiritual truths. Saintly halos, for instance, surround their heads, representing divine illuminescence and sanctity.

Moreover, the integral art pieces within Benedictine architecture present a veritable litany of symbols reflecting the spiritual doctrine left by Benedict and Scholastica. Intricate carvings of vines and branches lining the wooden stalls in choir lofts subtly remind monks of the parable of the vine and branches, a call for spiritual fruitfulness guided by the Rule. These tangible elements are grafts of holy wisdom planted in the very marrow of the monastic community.

The fusion of iconography and symbolism also plays a critical role in the sacred liturgy celebrated within Benedictine settings. Consider the altar, the celestial and terrestrial meeting point, where divine mysteries are enacted. The altar cloths, often embroidered with symbols such as the Chi-Rho or the Alpha and Omega, affirm not only Christ's sovereignty but Benedict's insistence on structuring life around divine worship.

Gardens, often meticulously maintained in Benedictine monasteries, also translate these iconographies into living, breathing parables. Herbs and flowers, chosen for their medicinal and symbolic properties, reflect both the care for creation and the healing vocation prescribed by monastic life. The intentional design of these gardens echoes the Edenic vision of harmony and offers a glimpse into the utopian ideal that these saints strive to embody.

The broader communities surrounding Benedictine institutions are not without influence from this rich tapestry of symbols. From wayside crosses marking pilgrim paths to statues adorning public squares, the reach of Benedictine symbolism extends far beyond the cloister walls. Each sacred image, each structurally austere yet theologically profound church exterior, serves as a cultural testament to the monastic world's enduring spiritual vitality.

Water, a central symbol in Christian sacramentality, holds special significance for the depiction of Saint Scholastica. Icons often show her by a spring or well, indicating her prayers summoning divine grace. This not only portrays her deep connection to God but aligns with the theme of water as a purifying and life-sustaining element. The metaphor of living water reflects the sanctifying influence she had on her community.

The historical persistence of these symbols serves as an allegorical mirror, reflecting the perennial influence of Saints Benedict and Scholastica. Mystical and practical dimensions weave together, creating a rich, multi-faceted narrative that transcends mere historical recounting. Each symbol is an invitation to delve deeper into the spiritual ethos that pervades Benedictine monastic life.

By engaging with the iconography and symbolism of Benedict and Scholastica, we partake in a greater liturgical and mystical tableau. The elements, whether in glorious cathedral settings or humble monastic chapels, compel the observer to unravel the layers of sacred tradition and lived sanctity that these holy siblings represent. Each symbol, each icon, is a testament to their enduring legacy, calling us toward higher spiritual aspirations and a more disciplined, sacramental life.

Chapter 13: Modern Interpretations of the Rule

In an age defined by relentless noise and constant connectivity, the Rule of Saint Benedict serves as an unexpected but profoundly necessary beacon for guiding the contemporary soul. While the medieval monastic ideal might seem worlds apart from today's digital age, the core principles of balance, prayer, and community find renewed relevance. Modern interpretations of the Rule adapt its timeless wisdom to fit a range of lifestyles: from the structured serenity of cloistered convents to the dynamic lives of laypeople seeking spiritual depth amid secular obligations. This dynamic adaptability emphasizes personal transformation and communal harmony, suggesting that despite the passage of centuries, the Rule's essence offers a countercultural balm to modern existential disarray. Through various retreats and Oblate programs, the Rule's call to a disciplined, contemplative life continues to resonate, inviting a diverse array of seekers to discover their own path to spiritual and moral integrity.

Adapting the Rule for Contemporary Life

Peering back through the mystical veils of history, the Rule of Saint Benedict stands not merely as a relic but as a luminous beacon guiding us through the complexities of contemporary life. Its ancient precepts may have been etched in an era of stark monasticism, yet they pulsate with a timeless relevance. As we delve into this exploration, we find that the Rule's core principles have the uncanny ability to transcend centuries, adapting themselves like living entities to the needs of modern society. It's almost as if Saint Benedict, foreseeing the labyrinthine challenges of futurity, embedded within his Rule a mutability, a capacity to evolve.

The Rule's foundation lies in its balance of **prayer**, **work**, and **community**. Initially conceived for monastic enclaves isolated from the temporal chaos of the world, these principles now invite interpretation for broader applicability. In today's fast-paced world, the call to a contemplative life can seem like an anachronism, a quaint echo of a distant past. Yet, when interwoven with the fabric of modern daily life, the Rule's emphasis on rhythmic prayer practices offers a sanctuary from the perpetual motion. Engaging in periodic moments of reflection, much like the canonical Hours, could provide spiritual sustenance amidst our relentless routines.

Work, once confined to the fields and scriptoria of monasteries, now takes on new shapes and forms. The Rule's emphasis on labor is at its core a call to purposeful activity. For contemporary adherents, this translates into a mindfulness that infuses even the most mundane tasks with spiritual significance. The idea is not to separate the sacred from the secular, but to sanctify the secular. Whether through artisanal craftsmanship, intellectual endeavors, or even digital ventures, the Rule encourages a ceaseless engagement with the labor that edifies both the individual and the community.

The notion of community, perhaps more critical now than ever, resonates profoundly within the Rule's text. In a world increasingly fragmented by digital media and virtual realities, the call to communal living fosters authentic human connections and mutual support. This does not necessitate literal cohabitation but rather a commitment to shared values and collective well-being. The Rule's emphasis on mutual obedience, respect, and accountability can transform our understanding of how to live harmoniously within diverse social and cultural landscapes. Benedictine wisdom inspires modern communities to cultivate spaces where individuals find belonging and purpose.

Moreover, the Rule's advocacy for moderation and discernment bespoke an ethical framework that holds invaluable lessons for contemporary life. In a society rife with excess and instant gratification, its call for balance and restraint serves as a countercultural manifesto. By advocating for a measured approach to consumption and desire, the Rule guides us towards sustainable and fulfilling living. Whether in personal habits or broader social structures, this exhortation to moderation provides a compass for navigating the moral and ethical dilemmas of our time.

Another significant aspect is the Rule's holistic view of education and intellectual pursuit. Initially applied within the confines of monastic education, this comprehensive approach can adapt seamlessly into modern educational paradigms. The focus on lifelong learning and intellectual humility can inspire students, educators, and lifelong learners alike, urging them to pursue knowledge not as an end but as a means to deeper wisdom and understanding. The Benedictine influence on education underscores the need for an integrative approach that harmonizes intellectual rigor with spiritual depth.

Nevertheless, adapting these ancient principles to the present era is not without its challenges. The Rule presupposes a level of commitment and discipline that may seem daunting to contemporary seekers. Yet, this very rigor can serve as a bulwark against the disorienting speed and superficiality of modern life. Simplifying and contextualizing the Rule's guidelines can make them accessible and applicable without losing their transformative power. Personal adaptation may involve setting realistic goals: nurturing a practice of weekly prayer or incorporating communal activities within one's social circles.

The technological advancements of the 21st century also bring unique opportunities for adapting the Rule. Digital platforms can facilitate virtual communities, where individuals separated by geography can gather for prayer, study, and mutual support. Online resources can provide access to spiritual exercises, monastic teachings, and communal interactions that enrich one's spiritual journey, thereby bringing the Rule's principles to a global audience.

The Rule's timelessness is evident in its inherent adaptability, addressing both individual transformation and communal nurture. In workplaces, it can inspire ethical leadership and collaborative cultures based on respect, accountability, and mutual support. Ecclesiastical communities can draw from its wisdom to foster inclusivity, spiritual growth, and social outreach. Families, too, can integrate these principles, creating environments where shared values and mutual care define daily interactions.

As we envision the future of Benedictine living, it becomes apparent that the Rule offers more than mere prescriptions; it provides a hermeneutic, a lens through which to view and engage with the world. This prophetic aspect of the Rule challenges and inspires us to explore deeper realms of both individual and collective potential. While honoring its historical context, we also unearth its prophetic voice that speaks eloquently into our contemporary conditions and crises.

Ultimately, the process of adapting the Rule for contemporary life is a creative and dynamic endeavor. It invites us to reimagine monastic wisdom in ways that resonate with our current experiences while remaining faithful to its core values. This balance between tradition and innovation ensures that Saint Benedict's vision continues to illumine our paths, guiding us towards holistic and sacred living amidst the dizzying complexities of modern life.

Thus, as we stand at the intersection of the ancient and the modern, the Rule of Saint Benedict unfolds before us not as a static document imprisoned by time but as a living testament to spiritual resilience and communal harmony. It is in this vibrant interplay of the ancient wisdom and contemporary relevance that the enduring legacy of Saint Benedict and Saint Scholastica continues to flourish, illuminating our journey through the ever-evolving tapestry of human life.

Chapter 14: Benedictine Oblates and Lay Associates

Benedictine Oblates and lay associates stand as living bridges between the cloistered world of the monastic community and the secular rhythms of everyday life. These individuals, committed to integrating the spiritual wisdom of Saint Benedict's Rule into their daily pursuits, exemplify the harmonious union of contemplation and action. Modern-day oblates, hailing from diverse walks of life, undertake a profound journey of spiritual formation that aligns closely with the monastic rhythm of prayer, work, and study, even while residing outside monastery walls. Their contributions extend far beyond mere support to monastic communities; they actively partake in the Benedictine mission of hospitality, service, and education. In embracing the Rule's principles, these lay associates serve as a testament to the enduring relevance of Benedictine spirituality, perpetuating the legacies of Saints Benedict and Scholastica in a world ever in need of spiritual grounding and moral clarity.

Role and Contributions of Lay People

The profound influence of lay people within the Benedictine tradition extends far beyond the cloistered walls of monastic life, shaping both spiritual and communal realms in ways that mirror a harmonious balance between the sacred and the secular. These individuals, known as Oblates or Lay Associates, embrace the Rule of Saint Benedict not through vows of celibacy or cloistering but by integrating its precepts into their daily lives. Their contributions manifest in numerous ways; they sustain monastic communities through practical support and moral encouragement, they embody Benedictine values in their professional and personal endeavors, and they serve as vital conduits for the tradition's teachings, ensuring its relevance in contemporary society. In this symbiotic relationship, the laity's external engagements fortify the spiritual disciplines of the monastics, presenting an allegory of a world where contemplation and action are deeply intertwined, each nourishing the other towards the greater good of both Church and society.

Modern-Day Oblates represent a fascinating and dynamic continuation of the Benedictine tradition. Rooted deeply in the monastic heritage established by Saints Benedict and Scholastica, these lay associates embody a contemporary manifestation of ancient spiritual principles. Oblates don't necessarily live within monastery walls; rather, they integrate the Rule of Saint Benedict into their everyday lives, transforming secular environments into spaces of contemplative action.

Unlike medieval oblates, who were often children dedicated to monastic life by their families, modern-day oblates are usually adults who choose this path out of a personal and spiritual calling. They may be single or married, professionals or retirees, yet all are united by a shared commitment to the monastic values of stability, obedience, and conversion of life. These guiding principles shape not only their spiritual practices but also their interactions with family, community, and work. It is as if the walls of the monastery extend into the world, bringing the sacred rhythms of monastic life into the heart of secular society.

Their spiritual journey often begins with an attraction to the Benedictine way of life, perhaps sparked by reading "The Rule of Saint Benedict" or through visiting a monastery. After a period of discernment and initial formation, prospective oblates undergo a formal commitment ceremony, binding themselves symbolically to a monastic community. This bond serves as a touchstone for their ongoing spiritual growth, supported by regular prayer, reading, and engagement with Benedictine texts.

Oblates are encouraged to maintain a balanced life, integrating times of prayer, work, and leisure, much like their monastic counterparts. They often have structured periods for morning and evening prayers, aligning their day with the liturgical hours. This rhythm fosters an atmosphere of continuous contemplation and spiritual attentiveness, even amidst the busyness of modern life. Through these practices, they become spiritual bridges, connecting the ancient wisdom of the monastic tradition with the needs and challenges of the present day.

While they live predominantly in the secular world, oblates maintain a deep, ongoing connection with their monastic communities. This relationship is nurtured through regular communication, visits, and participation in retreats and special liturgical celebrations. Some even take on specific roles within the monastery, assisting with various tasks or offering their professional skills. This symbiotic relationship enriches both the monastic and oblate communities, creating a vibrant exchange of spiritual and practical support.

In their professional and personal lives, modern oblates strive to embody Benedictine values such as humility, hospitality, and stewardship. This might manifest in various ways, from advocating for ethical business practices to fostering environments of inclusivity and respect. The oblate's commitment to "ora et labora" (prayer and work) inspires them to seek ways to bring holiness into the everyday, whether through mindful work, compassionate interactions, or dedicated service to others.

One of the unique aspects of the oblate vocation is its adaptability. The Rule of Saint Benedict offers timeless wisdom, yet it is open to interpretation and application within the context of contemporary living. Oblates creatively explore how these ancient practices can inform and transform modern challenges. For instance, in a world marked by digital overload and hurried activities, the Benedictine emphasis on mindfulness and presence becomes a countercultural act of resistance.

Technology, often seen as a distraction from spirituality, is approached differently by modern oblates. Many use it as a tool to sustain connections with their monastic community and fellow oblates, attending virtual retreats or engaging in online discussions about spiritual practice. This blend of ancient tradition with modern technology illustrates the dynamic and evolving nature of the oblate vocation, continually adapting to nurture the spiritual lives of its members.

Oblation is not a solitary endeavor. Community interaction plays a vital role, and oblates often form local or regional groups to support each other in their spiritual journeys. These gatherings, whether physical or virtual, provide spaces for shared prayer, study, and encouragement. They reflect the communal heart of the Benedictine tradition, reminding oblates that they are part of a broader spiritual family, both locally and globally.

Through their example, modern-day oblates offer a powerful witness to the relevance and vitality of Benedictine spirituality in the contemporary world. They show that the principles laid down by Saint Benedict over 1,500 years ago still have the power to shape lives, communities, and societies today. By living out these values in diverse contexts, oblates contribute to a broader understanding of what it means to be a bearer of the Benedictine spirit in the modern age.

Challenges inevitably arise. The demands of modern life can sometimes seem at odds with the contemplative ideals of monastic spirituality. Oblates must navigate these tensions, finding ways to maintain their spiritual commitments amidst professional responsibilities and family obligations. This balancing act requires discernment, flexibility, and a supportive community, both within the monastery and among fellow oblates.

Yet, it is precisely these challenges that make the journey of the modern-day oblate so enriching. In striving to live out Benedictine values in the world, oblates encounter opportunities for profound spiritual growth and transformation. They continually return to the central tenets of the Rule, finding in its ancient wisdom a guiding light for modern dilemmas. Thus, the life of an oblate becomes a pilgrimage, perpetually seeking to bring the sacred into the ordinary.

In conclusion, modern-day oblates represent a vibrant and evolving expression of Benedictine spirituality. They draw from the rich heritage of Saints Benedict and Scholastica, integrating these timeless principles into the fabric of contemporary life. Through their dedicated efforts, they serve as living bridges between the ancient monastic wisdom and the spiritual needs of today's world, embodying a timeless tradition in a modern context.

Chapter 15: Benedictine Monasteries Today

In the present era, Benedictine monasteries serve as enduring bastions of spiritual and communal life, carrying forward the ancient traditions laid down by Saints Benedict and Scholastica. These modern havens of tranquility often find themselves at a crossroads of preserving age-old practices while embracing contemporary challenges and opportunities. The monks and nuns within these monasteries continue to live by the Rule of Saint Benedict, adapting its timeless wisdom to address issues such as ecological sustainability, social justice, and interfaith dialogue. Life in these communities, though rigorous, pulses with a sense of purpose and devotion that harks back to monastic ideals. At the same time, these institutions engage with the broader world, offering retreats and educational programs that draw many seeking a deeper spiritual experience. Thus, Benedictine monasteries today encapsulate a delicate balance between steadfast adherence to foundational principles and the dynamic engagement with an ever-evolving society.

Contemporary Monastic Communities

In our times, contemporary monastic communities rooted in Benedictine tradition continue to serve as beacons of spiritual purity amidst an increasingly secular world. These communities, cloaked in the timeless garb of their vows, carve out sanctuaries from the ceaseless din of everyday life. Yet, their presence does not merely mark isolation from society; it embodies a paradoxical engagement with the world through prayer, labor, and hospitality. Each monastery operates as a microcosm of a utopian society, where every member, regardless of gender, embraces a harmonious balance of work and prayer, echoing the principles laid out by Saints Benedict and Scholastica. Through efforts in education, social justice, and environmental sustainability, these modern monastics uphold a living testament to their profound legacy, seamlessly weaving age-old wisdom into the fabric of today's ever-evolving human experience.

Challenges and Opportunities arise naturally in any community striving to adhere to lofty spiritual ideals while navigating the currents of worldly existence. For modern Benedictine monasteries, the interplay between these ancient precepts and contemporary realities presents both formidable trials and significant possibilities. The Rule of Saint Benedict, a document of exceptional wisdom, envisioned a community grounded in prayer, work, and mutual respect. Yet, as contemporary society shifts in pace and priorities, so too must these monastic communities evolve without sacrificing their core principles.

The first challenge for contemporary Benedictine monasteries lies in maintaining a balance between tradition and modernity. Monks and nuns are called to live out the centuries-old Rule within a world that increasingly favors the transient over the eternal. In a society marked by rapid technological advancements and quick access to information, the timeless practices of contemplation and manual labor might seem anachronistic. However, these very practices offer a counter-narrative to a frenetic world, presenting an opportunity for monasteries to be sanctuaries of peace and stability. The challenge lies in articulating and living out this alternative vision in a way that resonates with modern sensibilities without diluting the core essence of monastic life.

Yet, opportunities often lurk within challenges. For Benedictine communities, the growing desire among people for mindfulness and spiritual depth offers fertile ground for engagement. Many seek an escape from the relentless pace of modern life and find solace in monastic retreats and spiritual guidance. By opening their doors to laypeople seeking spiritual renewal, monasteries can both fulfill their mission of hospitality and ensure their financial sustainability. The Benedictine charism of "ora et labora" (pray and work) thus finds new expressions in modern contexts, providing a bridge between the ancient and the contemporary.

Economic sustainability is another significant challenge for contemporary Benedictine monasteries. The traditional means of self-support—agricultural work, artisanal crafts, and guesthouse hospitality—face competition from large-scale commercial enterprises. However, this economic challenge provides an opportunity for monasteries to innovate. Some have turned to sustainable agriculture and organic farming methods, appealing to the modern ethos of environmental stewardship. Others have expanded their artisanal offerings to include products that cater to niche markets interested in ethically-sourced goods. These economic ventures not only sustain the monasteries but also articulate a Benedictine response to contemporary issues like environmental degradation and ethical consumerism.

Another pivotal area of challenge and opportunity is the integration of technology into monastic life. While the Rule of Saint Benedict was written in a pre-digital age, its principles of moderation and community can guide the mindful adoption of technology. The challenge is to utilize technological tools without becoming enslaved to them, maintaining the priority of spiritual and communal life. Some monasteries have successfully harnessed the power of the internet to reach a broader audience, livestreaming liturgies and offering online spiritual resources. This digital evangelization can extend the Benedictine influence far beyond the cloister walls, making the wisdom of the Rule accessible to a global audience.

Community life itself presents ongoing challenges and opportunities. The Rule emphasizes stability, humility, and mutual service, which are counter-cultural values in a society that prizes individualism and transient commitments. For monasteries, the challenge is to foster a deep sense of communal belonging among their members while navigating the interpersonal dynamics that inevitably arise. However, these communal challenges also present opportunities for profound personal growth and spiritual formation. The monastic community, when functioning well, becomes a living witness to the possibility of a life ordered by divine rather than secular priorities.

The role of women in contemporary Benedictine monasticism poses another set of challenges and opportunities. Saint Scholastica, as a spiritual companion to Saint Benedict, set a precedent for the significant contributions of women to the Benedictine tradition. However, modern monasteries must navigate gender dynamics within the Church and broader society. Women's monasteries continue to offer unique insights and contributions to the monastic landscape, yet they often receive less visibility than their male counterparts. This presents an opportunity for greater advocacy and recognition of women's roles within the Benedictine family, echoing the egalitarian spirit of Saint Scholastica herself.

Inter-monastic cooperation also presents both challenges and opportunities. As the number of vocations to monastic life declines in certain regions, the necessity of fostering connections between monasteries becomes more pressing. This cooperation can take many forms, from shared liturgical celebrations to collaborative economic ventures. While logistical and cultural differences pose challenges, the potential for a richer, more interconnected monastic life offers exciting possibilities. Such cooperation can strengthen the Benedictine presence in regions where individual communities might struggle alone.

Lastly, the challenge of maintaining the relevance of the Rule in a rapidly changing world also opens up opportunities for meaningful dialogue with contemporary issues. The principles of the Rule—stability, humility, and the sanctity of work—resonate deeply in a world grappling with ecological crises, social inequalities, and existential despair. By articulating the timeless wisdom of the Rule in response to these modern crises, Benedictine monasteries can contribute significantly to broader societal conversations. This engagement presents an opportunity for monastic communities to be not only refuges of spiritual depth but also active participants in the world's healing.

In conclusion, the landscape of contemporary Benedictine monasticism is marked by a dynamic interplay of challenges and opportunities. While the pressures of modernity pose significant trials, they also offer unprecedented avenues for renewal and engagement. By staying rooted in their ancient tradition while innovatively responding to contemporary realities, Benedictine monasteries can continue to be beacons of stability, peace, and spiritual wisdom. This dual engagement ensures that the enduring legacy of Saints

Benedict and Scholastica remains vibrant and relevant, offering hope and guidance to a world in desperate need of both.

Chapter 16: The Ecumenical Legacy of Benedict and Scholastica

The legacy of Saints Benedict and Scholastica extends beyond the realms of their monastic communities, weaving a tapestry of unity and interfaith dialogue that resonates through the annals of history. Their lives and teachings laid the cornerstone for a harmonious coexistence among diverse religious traditions, bridging gaps and fostering mutual understanding. Benedict's Rule, with its emphasis on hospitality and humility, and Scholastica's unwavering devotion to community life, became beacons of inclusivity. This ecumenical spirit invited monks and laypeople alike to engage in acts of compassion and solidarity, promoting a universal ethos that transcends doctrinal boundaries. By pioneering a path of spiritual brotherhood and sisterhood, they left an indelible mark on the collective conscience, guiding countless souls towards a utopian vision of peace and cooperation. Their ecumenical influence is perhaps one of the most enduring aspects of their spiritual heritage, inviting contemporary believers and historians to reflect on the enduring power of unity in diversity.

Interfaith Dialogue and Cooperation

Saints Benedict and Scholastica have historically laid down the foundations not only for the spiritual lives of countless monks and nuns but also for fostering a wider understanding among differing faith traditions. Their legacy of interfaith dialogue and cooperation speaks volumes about their ability to influence spiritual and social frameworks well beyond their immediate context. Both siblings, although primarily committed to Christian monasticism, exhibited values that resonate universally, creating inroads into interfaith dialogues that have endured for centuries.

One could argue that the seeds of interfaith cooperation were sown through the inclusive and thoughtful precepts laid out in the Rule of Saint Benedict itself. The Rule emphasizes hospitality—"Let all guests who arrive be received like Christ"—which encourages monks to be open to strangers, irrespective of their faith. This spirit of openness becomes particularly relevant in our contemporary world, constantly fractured by religious and ideological boundaries. Scholastica's wisdom and inclusive spirit helped extend this attitude of acceptance and understanding further, making their monasteries places of refuge and intercultural dialogue.

During the medieval period, Benedictine monasteries often became sanctuaries where scholars from various religions met and engaged in meaningful dialogue. Texts from Islamic, Jewish, and Christian traditions were studied, translated, and debated within these walls, fostering an environment of intellectual and spiritual exchange. This interaction wasn't just academic; it humanized the "other" and built common ground, laying early frameworks for ecumenical and interfaith conversations.

Consider the dialogues between Christian and Islamic scholars during the Crusades. Despite the hostilities, monastic spaces sometimes served as neutral grounds where mutual respect and intellectual curiosity took precedence over conflict. Such instances of interfaith harmony underscore the Benedictine tradition's broader implications on international relations and cultural understanding—a tradition initially nurtured by the teachings of Benedict and Scholastica.

Delving deeper, one finds that their legacy influenced not just interactions between different religious traditions but also ideologies within Christianity itself. The harmonious relationship between Benedict and Scholastica symbolizes an aspirational unity, mirroring the ecumenical efforts among various Christian denominations. These efforts remind us that unity and diversity can coexist, this balance being essential for the endurance of any interfaith dialogue.

In modern times, Benedictine monasteries continue to uphold this legacy by fostering interfaith cooperation through programs and community initiatives. For instance, many monasteries host interfaith retreats and dialogues, creating platforms where people of different faith backgrounds can come together to discuss shared values and concerns. This modern application of ancient wisdom proves the timeless nature of what Benedict and

Scholastica have inspired: a pursuit of peace and unity through understanding and mutual respect.

The Rule of Saint Benedict, as implemented by communities today, greatly aids this mission. Its stress on humility, listening, and discernment becomes a guide for contemporary Benedictine communities engaging in interfaith work. Monks and laypeople alike are called to approach dialogues not with the intention of conversion but with genuine interest in listening and understanding—a subtle but profound extension of Benedict's directive to "listen with the ear of your heart."

It's also essential to note how their legacy impacts global issues like social justice and human rights. The monastic call to care for the 'other' transcends religious boundaries and finds itself in solidarity with various global movements committed to peace and justice. This holistic approach to interfaith cooperation further amplifies the relevance of Benedict and Scholastica's teachings in our interconnected world.

In this nuanced tapestry of interfaith dialogue and cooperation, the role of women, drawing inspiration from Scholastica, has been particularly significant. Scholastica's example empowers not just nuns but also laywomen to take active roles in these conversations, ensuring that interfaith engagements are enriched by diverse perspectives. Her role is a reminder that interfaith dialogue is not just a male enterprise but a human one, calling for equality and equity in all discussions.

Thus, the ecumenical legacy of Benedict and Scholastica is not confined to the boundaries of their era but echoes through history into the present. Their contributions provide a blueprint for interfaith endeavors, emphasizing mutual respect, intellectual curiosity, and spiritual kinship. Through their lives and teachings, they have illuminated pathways that lead not just to spiritual growth but to a larger, more inclusive understanding of humanity's shared spiritual journey.

Chapter 17: Benedictine Spirituality in Daily Life

Navigating the labyrinth of daily existence, one finds Benedictine spirituality not as an escape, but as a compass—integrating prayer, work, and community into a harmonious rhythm. For the modern Christian, Saint Benedict's wisdom is not confined within the cloisters of Monte Cassino; it beckons from every mundane task and every moment of contemplation. Here, the opus Dei, or the Work of God, echoes through our routines, urging us to sanctify every action with intention and presence. Through ora et labora, we weave a tapestry where the sacred and the secular interlace seamlessly, and community life extends beyond monastic walls, inviting us into a shared pilgrimage. In the footsteps of Benedict and Scholastica, we encounter a spirituality that grounds us in humility and elevates us through service, teaching us that in the simple acts, the divine becomes manifest.

Core Principles for Modern Christians

In our journey through the labyrinth of contemporary existence, the core principles of Benedictine spirituality offer a beacon of wisdom that transcends the constraints of time. Enshrined in the Rule of Saint Benedict, these tenets serve as the bedrock for modern Christians seeking a life that marries faith with the practicalities of daily living. The principle of "Ora et Labora" (Prayer and Work) guides us to harmonize our spiritual devotion with our worldly responsibilities, encouraging us to find divinity in both moments of quiet contemplation and in the labor of our hands. Stability and community, central to Benedict's teachings, urge us to foster collective well-being and spiritual growth within our communities, resisting the fragmentation of modern society. These enduring precepts, tested through centuries of monastic tradition, provide a timeless framework for embodying faith in an ever-changing world.

Prayer, Work, and Community have always been pivotal to understanding the engine that drives Benedictine spirituality. These elements are not mere components but rather interwoven strands that, bound together, create a robust fabric of life devoted to both the divine and the human experience.

Benedictine spirituality finds its roots in deep contemplation and deliberate action—a rhythm of life signaled by moments of prayer and intervals of diligent work. Prayer is not just a scheduled activity; it is life's breath, filling every action and every pause with purpose. Whether during the serene chanting of the Divine Office or in the silent whispers of individual prayer, every utterance and every silent beat carries the weight of divine conversation.

Benedict described this sense of perpetual dialogue with God as "ora et labora"—prayer and work. In Benedictine tradition, prayer encompasses more than the formalities of liturgy; it extends to an attitude of the heart, a constant orientation towards the divine. Consider the monk who, while tilling the soil, imbues each stroke of the hoe with a quiet prayer. In this blending of the sacred and the mundane, the Benedictine finds an echo of grace.

Just as crucial as prayer, work in Benedictine life transcends mere labor. It is an expression of devotion and community. Physical toil, whether in fields or workshops, becomes a medium that sanctifies the day. The sweat of the brow is not just effort spent but a symbol of the soul's striving towards holiness. Labor grounds the ethereal nature of prayer, rooting it in the earth and in human reality.

The community, something Benedict envisioned as a family bound not by blood but by spiritual kinship, becomes an arena where both prayer and work play out. Here, the collective experience fortifies the individual's resolve, creating a unity that is as much spiritual as it is practical. Each member of the community supports the other, pooling resources, talents, and prayers into a singular effort that magnifies the divine aspiration of the whole.

Within the community, there is a remarkable balancing act between communal life and individual responsibility. While the Rule of Saint Benedict strictly delineates times for prayer, work, and even rest, it never loses sight of the individual's spiritual journey. Personal virtues and community harmony coalesce, allowing each monk or nun to find their unique path within the larger collective.

This balance of prayer, work, and community offers a lens through which modern society can explore its own dynamics. In an era marked by disconnection and individualism, the Benedictine model exemplifies a harmonious integration of roles—a symphony where each note, whether struck in the field or sung in the choir, contributes to the overarching melody of sacred living.

Imagine the stone carver, chiseling away in the monastery's workshop. Each strike of the hammer resonates not only as an act of creation but as a prayer, connecting the carver to the divine artisan. In this labor, the boundary between sacred and profane dissolves, illustrating the Benedictine ethos where work itself becomes a liturgy.

Even within the constraints of communal life, there remains ample room for the flourishing of personal talents and vocations. Whether crafting manuscripts, tending to gardens, or engaging in scholarly pursuits, each task is embraced as a unique offering to the divine and the community. This inclusivity—of skill, of talent, of calling—strengthens the communal fabric, making each member indispensable.

The Rule's emphasis on mutual service and respect fosters a culture where every individual, regardless of their role, is valued. This not only elevates the act of work but instills a sacred dignity in daily labor, reframing it as a crucial element of spiritual practice rather than mere economic necessity. In a world increasingly obsessed with material gain and personal ambition, Benedictine work reintroduces the notion of labor as divine service.

One might ponder the evenings in a Benedictine abbey. As the day winds down and Vespers echo through the cloister, there is a palpable sense of completion. The community gathers, drawn together by the twin strands of prayer and work that have woven their day. This rhythm—this cyclical dance of toil and tranquility—shapes not just the monastic day but the monastic soul.

Community itself becomes a crucible where spiritual growth is tested and tempered. Living in close quarters with others requires a humility that is continually exercised. Pride is a weed quickly uprooted by the relentless demands of communal living, where each person's success is bound to everyone else's. The Rule, with its prescriptions for mutual care and correction, ensures that no one is left to flounder in their spiritual journey alone.

Saint Benedict's design for community life was as pragmatic as it was spiritual. He foresaw potential conflicts and addressed them preemptively within the Rule, urging monks to bear with one another's weaknesses and to support one another's strengths. He mandated roles that rotated, ensuring no task became monotonous or overly burdensome for any individual. This careful structuring prevented the isolation of the individual while fostering a robust community spirit.

The apostolic life envisioned by Benedict is an enduring testament to the power of collective effort and shared purpose. It stands as an enduring model of how human beings may organize themselves not just for survival or prosperity, but for sanctification. The monastery, with its balance of prayer, work, and community, becomes a microcosm of a possible ideal society.

For historians, the study of Benedictine community life offers more than just a glimpse into monastic routines; it reveals the underlying principles that can guide any societal organization towards greater harmony and purpose. And for Roman Catholics, it provides a living example of how to weave one's personal spiritual journey into the broader tapestry of communal faith.

Thus, prayer, work, and community are not just tenets but intertwined threads that form the unbroken cord of Benedictine monasticism. Each element strengthens the other, creating a complete and harmonious way of life that has endured through centuries, offering wisdom and solace to all who seek it. The Rule encapsulates this balance, serving as both a guide and an inspiration for how to live in the world yet beyond it, anchored in both action and contemplation.

Chapter 18: Pilgrimage and Veneration of Saints Benedict and Scholastica

The journey to venerate Saints Benedict and Scholastica, a pilgrimage undertaken by many faithful, becomes a profound quest bridging the physical and spiritual realms. Pilgrims often find themselves drawn to the sacred grounds of Monte Cassino, where the echoes of Benedict's wisdom and Scholastica's devotion resonate through time. These sacred sites, infused with history and divine presence, offer not just a physical destination but a spiritual beacon. The act of pilgrimage itself transforms the seeker, where each step symbolizes a journey deeper into faith, contemplation, and communal solidarity. The veneration of these saints, rooted in their exemplary lives and enduring legacies, provides pilgrims with a model of holy living, inspiring them to embody virtues of humility, obedience, and fraternal love. This pilgrimage thus emerges as a testament to the enduring power of Benedictine spirituality, seamlessly weaving the past's sacred traditions with the present's fervent devotion.

Popular Pilgrimage Sites

Traversing the mystical paths of faith, pilgrims have long been drawn to the sacred grounds associated with Saints Benedict and Scholastica, yearning for spiritual nourishment and historical connection. Monte Cassino, the cradle of the Benedictine order, stands as the epicenter of this pilgrimage, a hallowed sanctuary whispering tales of perseverance and devotion. The site's restoration after wartime devastation has only deepened its symbolic resonance, embodying both the fragility and resilience of spiritual fortitude. Beyond Monte Cassino, lesser-known yet equally revered sites like Subiaco and Norcia weave together the physical and metaphysical, offering pilgrims an intricate tapestry of holiness and heritage. These sanctified destinations echo with the timeless virtues imparted by the brother and sister saints, beckoning the faithful to engage with a legacy marked by both pastoral simplicity and profound theological depth.

Monte Cassino and Beyond reveals not just a place of bricks and stones but a fountainhead of spirituality, intellectual vigor, and timeless traditions that flowed from Saint Benedict's vision. The perching of Monte Cassino atop its hill unveils less of a solitary fortress and more of a beacon that casts an enduring light across the ages. This section peers into the layers of history and spirituality associated with Monte Cassino, illuminating the broader legacy of Benedictine principles and the ongoing pilgrimage that seeks out this hallowed ground.

The foundation of Monte Cassino brought forth an era marked by a disciplined yet adaptable approach to monastic life, embodying the Rule Saint Benedict had meticulously crafted. This Rule, with its focus on "ora et labora" (pray and work), found fertile ground at Monte Cassino, allowing the seeds of a lively yet orderly community to sprout and flourish. It became a living manuscript of prayer, study, and labor, each leaf turned by the monks punctuating time with chants, toil, and contemplation.

But Monte Cassino's significance didn't confine itself within monastic walls. As a venerated site, it drew pilgrims from different spheres of life, knitting a tapestry of varied souls all seeking something transcendent. Many came seeking solace, eternal insights, or just a brush with the divine. They left, not just having touched hallowed relics or viewed austere stonework but often carrying away a deeper spiritual resonance that would echo in their everyday lives.

Beyond its sacred corridors, the influence of Monte Cassino spread like tributaries feeding a river of renewal and scholarly excellence across Europe. Its monks copied and preserved ancient manuscripts, bridging the past and future, safeguarding knowledge when the continent's intellectual landscape was often in peril. These efforts went "beyond" the monastery, touching universities, libraries, and scholars far removed from its immediate sphere, ensuring that erudition would continue to enlighten minds long after the sun set over the hill.

Monte Cassino also became a harbinger of art and architecture, projecting a vision of divine harmony. The iconic church designs, the rich symbolism embedded in frescoes and mosaics within its precincts, reflected theological principles and the Benedictine way of life. It wasn't merely about the aesthetic; it was about embodying the sacred in the tangible, turning stone and pigment into vessels of divine truth and human aspiration.

In the tapestry of monastic reform, Monte Cassino held its fibers tightly. Whether in response to internal slackness or external pressures, it stood as a bastion of renewal, demonstrating that true fidelity to monastic principles often required dynamic adaptation without succumbing to transient trends. Through various waves of reform—whether Cluniac, Cistercian, or later movements—the ethos of Monte Cassino's disciplined yet adaptable framework persisted as a guiding star.

The devotion to Saints Benedict and Scholastica has remained vibrant and perennial, as their lives exemplified virtues that have perennial relevance. Pilgrims today tread these sacred paths to Monte Cassino, not merely in homage, but in a quest for the timeless wisdom sculpted into the soul of Benedictine spirituality. While the abbey has been ravaged by wars and rebuilt through the centuries, its spiritual edifice stands unwavering, a testament to the enduring human longing for divine communion and holy companionship.

As we ponder "Monte Cassino and Beyond," it becomes clear that its essence can't be constrained to physical boundaries. The reach of its spirituality and intellectual heritage extends into the very fabric of Western civilization. From educational systems founded on monastic principles to the preservation of classical knowledge, Monte Cassino's ripple effect is both profound and extensive. The journey of its influence threads through centuries, transcending the constraints of time and geography.

Thus, Monte Cassino finds a place not just on the maps of geography but in the contours of the heart and the realms of the mind. Its legacy is ever-evolving, morphing from one generation to the next, ever ancient and ever new. The pilgrimage continues, both literally to its sacred site and metaphorically in the application of Benedictine principles in modern contexts. The spirit of "ora et labora" that animates Monte Cassino breathes life into endeavors of contemporary Benedictine communities and lay associates, ensuring that this hallowed hill's beacon remains lit for those who yearn for its guiding light.

Whether in times of peace or amidst the clamor of rebuilding from calamity, Monte Cassino's walls have continued to reverberate with the chants of monks, their voices rising like incense, testifying to a faith that endures. The resilience of this spiritual citadel teaches us that no matter the storm, the essence of what it means to be a community of faith and intellectual pursuit cannot be washed away but rather stands firm, drawing strength from its roots in Saint Benedict's transformative vision.

As we move beyond the confines of Monte Cassino, we carry its teachings, its spirit, and its example into our own lives and communities. The principles set forth by Saints Benedict and Scholastica constitute a legacy that remains relevant, providing a pathway to balance, harmony, and integrity. Their sanctuary, initially a refuge from a world in turmoil, has evolved into a beacon guiding numerous souls through the centuries, compelling us to ask how we might integrate these enduring principles into the modern ebb and flow of life.

In reflecting upon "Monte Cassino and Beyond," one cannot help but realize that the heartbeat of this sacred site echoes throughout the world. It's felt in the quiet of personal prayer, the bustling activity of charity work, the silent labor of scholars, and the collective efforts of communities seeking a higher purpose. This place, with its rich history and unyielding spiritual presence, continues to inspire and guide, much like the eternal flame it represents.

Chapter 19: Impact on Western Culture

The profound legacy of Saints Benedict and Scholastica permeates the very fabric of Western culture, weaving threads of spiritual discipline, intellectual rigor, and communal ethos. Their influence, encapsulated primarily through the Rule of Saint Benedict, established a foundation for monastic life that reverberated far beyond the cloisters of Monte Cassino. This Rule, advocating balance, prayer, and labor, became a cornerstone for educational and religious institutions, fostering a culture of preservation and transmission of knowledge during tumultuous times. Moreover, their balanced approach to faith and reason nourished the seeds of Western philosophical thought, echoing in the halls of medieval universities and the works of scholars who sought to integrate spiritual and temporal wisdom. Thus, Benedictine principles transcended their monastic origins, indelibly shaping Western moral and intellectual traditions.

Cultural and Intellectual Contributions

Saints Benedict and Scholastica, both individually and collectively, had far-reaching influences that transcended their immediate religious communities. Their contributions to Western culture and intellectual thought are profound and enduring, shedding light on principles that have continued to shape societal and cultural norms for centuries.

Saint Benedict, often hailed as the father of Western monasticism, laid the foundations for a disciplined and communal way of life that affected not just religious practices but also influenced Western thought and culture. The *Rule of Saint Benedict* codified a balanced approach to work, prayer, and study that not only became a cornerstone for monastic life but also permeated the broader culture. These precepts propagated a vision of community and shared purpose that encouraged intellectual and cultural advancements within and beyond the cloistered walls of the monasteries.

The Benedictine monasteries themselves became centers of learning and culture during the Middle Ages. As places of education, these institutions were pivotal in preserving classical texts and fostering the intellectual climate that fueled the Carolingian Renaissance. The practice of copying manuscripts was more than mere preservation; it was a dedication to the continuity of knowledge. The precise and disciplined work of Benedictine scribes ensured that the wisdom of antiquity was carried into the future, paving the way for the educational and philosophical transformations of the later Middle Ages and the Renaissance.

Besides preserving classical knowledge, Benedictine monastic schools contributed to the intellectual ferment by generating new scholastic insights and theological developments. These schools were the incubators of medieval thought, where logic, philosophy, and theology were rigorously pursued. The Benedictine commitment to stability, scribal exactitude, and scholarly pursuit infused Western intellectual traditions with a unique blend of faith and reason.

Saint Scholastica's influence, though often overshadowed by her brother's, was equally significant. She embodied and promoted the role of women in early Christian intellectual and spiritual life. While much of the historical narrative often focuses on male figures, Scholastica's impact cannot be ignored. Her spiritual leadership challenged and expanded the understanding of gender roles within the monastic context. By asserting a place for women in contemplative and communal religious practices, she subtly rewrote the intellectual and cultural script, advocating for a more inclusive spiritual and intellectual life.

Furthermore, the theological dialogues and spiritual exchange between Benedict and Scholastica served as an intellectual symbiosis, illustrating the Benedictine value of mutual support and learning. Their relationship becomes a microcosm for understanding the broader cultural synthesis that occurred in the monasteries: a blending of spiritual fervor with intellectual rigor, all underpinned by communal bonds.

The Benedictine emphasis on "Ora et Labora" (prayer and work) introduced a balanced approach to life that influenced broader societal values. This ethos permeated the culture, laying groundwork for what we may now recognize as the Protestant work ethic, centuries before its formal articulation. The commitment to both manual and intellectual labor, combined with a deeply meditative and contemplative spiritual practice, created a holistic view of human endeavors that transcended monastic boundaries. It balanced the sacred with the mundane, influencing the ethos of European cultural life.

This approach didn't just impact individuals within the monastery; it had a ripple effect throughout medieval Europe. The stabilizing influence of monasteries, grounded in Benedictine principles, often extended into the surrounding communities. These monks and nuns provided education, healthcare, and agricultural advancements to local populations. They became vital nodes of cultural and intellectual life, created spaces of continuity, and offered structure in an often fractured and turbulent medieval world.

Moreover, the architectural contributions of the Benedictine order can't be overlooked. The design and construction of monastic buildings, with their emphasis on harmony, functionality, and spirituality, mirrored the intellectual and cultural aspirations of the time. These architectural innovations would go on to influence Gothic and Romanesque styles, leaving a lasting imprint on Western ecclesiastical and secular architecture. The balance of form and function in monastic design reflects the Benedictine ideal of creating spaces that nourish both body and soul, an architectural manifestation of their holistic view of life.

Beyond just physical contributions, the intellectual exchanges promoted by Benedictine constructs facilitated early forms of multiculturalism and dialogue within Europe. Monastic libraries became repositories of not just Christian texts but also works from Jewish, Islamic, and pagan traditions. This inclusivity reflects a broader intellectual curiosity and openness, suggesting that the Benedictine pursuit of knowledge wasn't restricted by cultural or religious boundaries. The cross-pollination of ideas within these sacred spaces contributed significantly to the intellectual sophistication of Western Europe.

Additionally, the Benedictine influence stretched into art and iconography. The illuminated manuscripts produced in Benedictine scriptoriums were not just texts to be read but visual milestones that contributed to the Western artistic canon. These manuscripts featured intricate artwork that combined religious symbolism with artistic excellence, serving both as works of devotion and as historical artifacts that influenced Western art and aesthetics.

The Benedictine approach to music also left an indelible mark. Chanting the Divine Office required a level of musical skill and devotion that preserved and propagated Gregorian chant, which remains a cornerstone of Western liturgical music. The establishment of a structured, repetitive, and meditative approach to communal singing contributed to the aesthetic and spiritual dimensions of Western music, bridging the sacred and artistic worlds.

The lasting intellectual contributions of the Benedictine way of life are also manifested in their ethical and philosophical teachings. The balanced approach to discipline, combined with an appreciation for both silence and dialogue, contributed to the moral and philosophical underpinnings of Western Christianity and secular ethics. Their teachings about the virtues of humility, obedience, and community continue to influence Western ethical frameworks, demonstrating the profound and enduring impact of Benedictine thought on Western moral philosophy.

The legacy of Saints Benedict and Scholastica is thus a tapestry woven from threads of spiritual devotion, intellectual pursuit, and cultural contributions. Their twin paths of holiness and wisdom fostered a wellspring of ideas, artistic expressions, and societal structures that remain relevant to this day. The cultural and intellectual contributions they made to Western society are multifaceted, extending from the quietude of monastic scriptoriums to the grandeur of medieval cathedrals, from the minutiae of daily monastic routines to the broader cultural ethos of an entire civilization.

In the grand narrative of Western culture, the role of Benedictine monasticism stands as a testament to the power of lived philosophy and communal intellectual endeavor. The contributions of these saints to cultural and intellectual life are not mere historical footnotes; they are foundational pillars that continue to support and inspire the edifice of Western civilization. By blending the spiritual with the intellectual, the personal with the communal, Saints Benedict and Scholastica left an indelible imprint, a legacy that encourages continuous reflection, learning, and cultural growth.

Chapter 20: Benedictines in Education

The Benedictines have long stood as torchbearers of education within the framework of ecclesiastical and secular knowledge. Their profound commitment to learning is not merely ancillary but central to their monastic calling and societal role. By establishing monastic schools and later universities, they cultivated centers of intellectual rigor and spiritual growth. These institutions became beacons of hope and enlightenment during tumultuous eras, preserving classical texts and fostering a rich intellectual tradition. The legacy of Benedictine education reshaped the landscape of higher learning, embedding within it the virtues of discipline, contemplation, and community. Through their enduring influence, the Benedictines have enshrined the pursuit of wisdom as both a divine vocation and a civic duty, exemplifying how faith and reason coexist harmoniously.

Founding of Schools and Universities

Emerging from the hallowed walls of monastic life, the Benedictines established schools and universities that stand as luminous beacons of learning and virtue. Their pursuits were not mere dissemination of secular knowledge but rather a harmonious symphony blending divine wisdom with earthly understanding. The Benedictines, drawing from Saint Benedict's Rule, envisioned an educational paradigm where the cultivation of intellectual and spiritual growth was paramount. Through the founding of these institutions, they sought to create sanctuaries of scholarship, where the pursuit of truth could flourish and the soul could ascend towards the divine. In these centers of academia, education became an act of worship, and learning a pathway to salvation, setting a precedent for universities that continue to mold minds and spirits across generations.

Legacy in Higher Education The legacy of Saints Benedict and Scholastica finds profound expression in the realm of higher education. Their influence, though subtle in some quarters, has left an indelible mark on the structure, philosophy, and spirit of many educational institutions. To grasp this impact, we need to consider both the historical foundations laid by the Benedictine monastic schools and the perpetuation of Benedictine principles in contemporary educational systems.

Benedictine monasticism catalyzed the development of educational institutions from their inception. The Benedictine emphasis on discipline, structured learning, and community-centric living formed the pedagogical frameworks within medieval monastic schools, which evolved to become some of the earliest universities. These institutions were sanctuaries of knowledge where the Rule of Saint Benedict's principles shaped both the acquisition and dissemination of learning. The union of intellectual pursuit with spiritual devotion created an environment where each supported the other, fostering a holistic approach to education.

The concept of the 'schola' within the Benedictine monasteries cannot be overstated. These "schools" were more than mere centers of rote learning; they were places where the physical, intellectual, and spiritual development of a person was intertwined. The monks' diligent work in the scriptorium, copying and preserving manuscripts, not only safeguarded ancient knowledge but also encouraged an intellectual rigor that became the hallmark of monastic scholarship. This blending of manual labor and intellectual effort established a prototype for modern universities' balance between theory and practice.

The Rule of Saint Benedict articulated values that continue to resonate in the halls of higher education today. Stability, humility, and obedience were not just monastic virtues but became academic principles. Stability fostered a commitment to the academic community, humility encouraged an openness to learning, and obedience instilled a respect for scholarly tradition and authority. Together, they nurtured a pedagogical climate conducive to deep reflection and lifelong learning.

Furthermore, the emphasis on 'ora et labora'—prayer and work—fostered an educational ethos where contemplative life did not detract from academic pursuits but enhanced them. This integration of the spiritual and secular created a distinctive educational philosophy. Indeed, one finds that many modern universities rooted in Benedictine tradition maintain a unique balance between rigorous academic programs and the spiritual development of their students. This holistic approach has profoundly influenced the mission statements and educational strategies within these institutions.

One cannot ignore the pivotal role of Benedictine monasteries in preserving classical texts and fostering intellectual inquiry during times when Europe faced significant turmoil. Their academies laid the groundwork for European humanism—a return to classical sources and the application of rational inquiry that is central to modern Western education. This humanistic influence persists in the liberal arts education model, which remains profoundly shaped by the Benedictine commitment to the formative aspects of education.

The libraries of Benedictine monasteries were wondrous repositories of knowledge. Within the walls of Monte Cassino and similar monasteries, texts from antiquity were copied, studied, and taught. This dedication to learning and preservation played a crucial role in the later intellectual revival during the Renaissance. The roots of contemporary higher education institutions can often be traced back to these Benedictine traditions which placed great emphasis on both scholarly integrity and the moral development of the learner.

Moreover, the Benedictine legacy manifests in the architectural designs of universities with origins in these traditions. The quadrangles, cloisters, and calm spaces found within many campuses were inspired by monastic layouts, designed to create environments conducive to contemplation and study. The physical design of these institutions, reflecting the orderly and disciplined life advocated by the Rule, continues to influence campus architecture aimed at fostering community and reflection.

Benedictine contributions did not halt with the monastic scholae. During the height of the medieval period, many Benedictine scholars ventured beyond their monasteries to teach at burgeoning universities, such as those in Paris, Bologna, and Oxford. Their pedagogical methods, rigorous scholarship, and disciplined lifestyle set standards within fledgling academic communities. The fusion of liturgical, ethical, and intellectual traditions laid the groundwork for these universities' statutes and curricula, leaving a legacy that endures in their scholarly and communal ethos.

Today, Benedictine universities still thrive globally, a testament to the enduring power of the Benedictine approach to education. Institutions like Saint John's University in Minnesota and Benedictine College in Kansas illustrate how the principles of the Rule adapt to modern educational needs while staying rooted in their historical and spiritual heritage. These universities emphasize values such as community, stewardship, and service—echoing the enduring legacies of Saints Benedict and Scholastica.

Moreover, the Benedictine spirit of 'conversatio morum' or fidelity to monastic practices continues to inform the ethos of Benedictine educational institutions. This commitment to ongoing conversion and transformation, rooted in the monastic tradition, encourages students to engage not just in academic endeavors but in personal, spiritual, and moral growth. It is this transformative educational philosophy that reinforces the ideals of holistic personal development—arguably the most significant legacy Benedictine education imparts on higher education.

One can see the influence of the Benedictine commitment to communal living in modern residential colleges within universities, which foster close-knit communities where students live and learn together. This model, emphasizing mutual support and shared values, mirrors the monastic community life and encourages a form of collective engagement that enriches the educational experience.

Thus, the profound legacy of Saints Benedict and Scholastica in higher education lies in the enduring principles they championed. Their holistic approach to education, founded on the integration of intellectual, spiritual, and communal living, continues to shape institutions committed to nurturing well-rounded individuals ready to contribute meaningfully to society. In every monastic-inspired curriculum and community-centered campus, and in every student who lives out these principles, the spirit of Benedictine education thrives.

Chapter 21: Social Teachings and Justice

Saints Benedict and Scholastica's legacy doesn't just linger within the cloistered walls of monastic life; it permeates social structures, advocating justice and communal support. Their teachings unfurled a vision where the principles of prayer, labor, and mutual care transformed into a broader, utopian moral community, standing starkly against the dystopian facets of societal neglect and injustice. Benedict's Rule, with its insistence on the humane treatment of all members, extended an allegorical hand to wider society, emphasizing the fundamental tenets of equity, service, and advocacy for the marginalized. Scholastica, equally, imparted a maternal wisdom, nurturing the seeds of compassion and inclusivity. This intertwined doctrine, fashioned from the philosophical fibers of their lives, continues to resonate through historical and modern lenses, inspiring profound contributions to social work and advocacy, heralding a world anchored in justice and fraternity.

Advocacy and Social Work

The lives of Saints Benedict and Scholastica illuminate the profound confluence of advocacy and social work within the framework of Benedictine monasticism. Their holistic approach to justice was not limited to spiritual realms alone but extended fervently into the societal fabric, emphasizing actions over mere contemplation. In an era defined by hierarchical imbalance, they championed the needy and marginalized, ensuring that the divine imperative of charity manifested in every act. This was not a utopian ideal but a pragmatic vision of a harmonious community where labor and prayer intertwined seamlessly to uplift the downtrodden. Through their enduring legacy, we discern an allegory of relentless compassion—a timeless testament to the might of humble service and the indomitable pursuit of social justice rooted in spiritual conviction.

Historical and Modern Perspectives capture both the evolving legacy and the timeless relevance of Saints Benedict and Scholastica. These two exemplars of spiritual dedication, whose lives and works continue to influence Christian monasticism and beyond, have left an indelible mark on history. Their visions, rooted in the ascetic practices of early Christianity, evolved into guiding frameworks for communal religious living, shaping not just religious life but societal values. Modern perspectives, while basking in the glow of their historical contributions, add dimensions that speak to contemporary challenges and aspirations.

The journey of Saints Benedict and Scholastica begins in the 5th and 6th centuries, a time of great upheaval across Europe. The Roman Empire was crumbling, and societal chaos threatened the spiritual and temporal coherence that had long prevailed. It was in this context that Benedict and Scholastica pursued paths of spiritual asceticism. Benedict's life at Monte Cassino, crafting the Rule that would anchor the life of countless monastics, stands as a testament to his organizational genius and spiritual vision. Scholastica, often less heralded, nonetheless played a vital role as a spiritual counterpart and advisor to her brother.

As the centuries progressed, the Rule of Saint Benedict served as a bulwark of stability and learning. Medieval Europe saw the proliferation of Benedictine monasteries, which became centers of agriculture, education, and scholarship. These monasteries preserved not just religious texts but became the keepers of classical knowledge through their diligent copying of manuscripts. Historians often credit Benedictine monasteries with the survival of Western culture during times when Europe faced repeated invasions and internal strife. The rhythm of prayer, work, and contemplation that characterized Benedictine life provided a counterbalance to the fragmentation seen in broader society.

Fast forward to the modern era, and the Rule of Saint Benedict remains pertinent. Contemporary Christians find in it a set of principles that address modern existential challenges - the need for community, the search for balance between labor and leisure, and the quest for deeper spiritual fulfillment. The concepts of "stability" and "conversion of life" resonate even today, particularly in a world marked by rapid change and fleeting commitments. Benedictine monasteries today may have transformed, but they stand as enclaves of continuity, offering solace and guidance to those who seek it.

Modern perspectives also highlight how the Rule has adapted to contemporary life. Benedictine communities often engage in social work, uphold ecological stewardship, and contribute to the ongoing dialogue about faith and reason. The holistic approach to life outlined in the Rule - encompassing physical labor, intellectual pursuit, and spiritual devotion - finds new expressions in initiatives ranging from education to healthcare. Benedictines have been at the forefront of addressing issues like homelessness and climate change, revealing how the ancient ethos can be a force for modern good.

Moreover, the influence of the Rule extends beyond monastic walls. Lay people, inspired by the principles of Benedictine spirituality, form what are known as Benedictine oblates.

These associates commit to integrating the Rule's precepts into their daily lives while remaining in the secular world. Their existence underscores the universal application of Benedictine wisdom - a blueprint for how to live thoughtfully and intentionally in any circumstance. Through prayer, work, and communal involvement, these modern-day adherents echo the transformative legacies of Benedict and Scholastica.

But let's return momentarily to the narrative thread of history. The diffusion of Benedictine practices during the medieval period reshaped not just religious institutions but also societal structures. Monastic reforms, such as those initiated by the Cluniacs, originated from Benedictine principles but sought to purify and renew the spiritual rigor of monastic life. These reforms illustrate the dynamic interplay between tradition and renewal, a theme that resonates through subsequent generations.

Intriguingly, the insights of Saints Benedict and Scholastica also inform ecumenical dialogue. By returning to the foundational elements of Christian practice embodied in the Rule, strands of unity emerge among diverse Christian traditions. For example, Benedictine principles emphasize humility and hospitality—values that can bridge doctrinal divides and foster interfaith cooperation. Such engagements breathe new life into the ancient texts, showing how the wisdom of the past can illuminate paths for future harmony.

So, how can we measure the impact of Saints Benedict and Scholastica in today's world? Perhaps it lies in the enduring relevance of their teachings in addressing perennial human concerns. Their visions, which originally took shape to combat the societal disintegration and spiritual confusion of their time, still offer coherent strategies to navigate our own complex modernity. Whether through monastic commitment or lay engagement, the Rule provides a framework for a balanced, meaningful life, underscoring that ancient wisdom is not antiquated but perpetually applicable.

The conceptual bridge from historical to modern perspectives is robust, grounded in a timeless quest for spiritual and communal coherence. The enduring appeal of Benedictine spirituality lies in its balanced approach to life - an integration of prayer, work, and study. This tripartite framework offers an antidote to the fragmentation of contemporary existence, lending coherence to life's myriad demands. While societal contexts have evolved, the core human quest for stability, connection, and purpose remains unchanged.

In the legacy of Saints Benedict and Scholastica, we find a roadmap for navigating both historical complexities and modern dilemmas. Their Rule, a testament to communal living and spiritual discipline, transcends the ages, speaking to both the historian delving into the past and the modern seeker yearning for direction in an ever-changing world. Their storied lives and unwavering principles remind us that, amidst the tumult of history and the flux of modernity, there remain guiding stars illuminating the path to a meaningful and impactful life.

Chapter 22: The Rule and Contemporary Catholicism

The Rule of Saint Benedict, an intricate tapestry of spiritual principles and pragmatic guidelines, remains a vital pillar within Contemporary Catholicism. Embodying a harmonious blend of ascetic discipline and communal harmony, the Rule transcends its monastic origins, seeping into the broader ecclesial consciousness. Today, Catholic educators, clergy, and lay believers draw from its depths, seeking to infuse modern life with its timeless wisdom. Saint Benedict's vision of stability, obedience, and conversion of life serves not merely as an archaic relic but rather as a beacon guiding contemporary spiritual and moral endeavors. Its emphasis on balanced living—encapsulated in the famous Benedictine motto "Ora et Labora" (Pray and Work)—lends itself to the multifaceted challenges and opportunities facing the modern Church. Through this enduring framework, the Rule not only anchors individuals in their spiritual quests but also fosters a revitalized sense of community and purpose, resonating profoundly in the hearts of those striving for a life marked by faith and virtue in today's ever-changing world.

Integration into Modern Church Teachings

The ancient insights found in the Rule of Saint Benedict find an echo in the heart of contemporary Catholic teachings, much like a quiet river that courses through the centuries. The Rule, initially intended for monastic life, embodies wisdom that transcends the cloister walls, making it applicable to the broader church and its followers. The spiritual and philosophical import of Benedict's precepts weaves into the fabric of today's Catholic ethos, providing a timeless compass for those seeking harmony with divine will.

One of the remarkable aspects of the Rule is its emphasis on balance — a principle that has become increasingly necessary in our fast-paced and often fragmented modern lives. The triad of "Ora et Labora et Lectio" (Pray, Work, and Read) encapsulates a model for lived holiness, extending its beauty and utility far beyond monastic confines. In today's Church, this triadic structure offers a template for integrating spiritual practices with everyday tasks, fostering a holistic approach to faith. The synchronization of prayer, work, and intellectual engagement is not relegated to monks alone; it is a call to all Catholics to create a rhythm in their lives that align with divine order.

The Rule's contemplative essence emphasizes listening, not only to the words of Scripture but also to the voices within our communities and our hearts. This aligns seamlessly with the contemporary Church's stress on pastoral care and active listening. As Pope Francis often reminds us, the Church should be a "field hospital," a place where people come to be heard and healed. Benedict's advocacy for communal discernment and humility reinforces the Church's mission to engage with and uplift those on the periphery. It prompts both clergy and laity to adopt a posture of attentiveness and compassion, vital for authentic ecclesial engagement in a fractured world.

Moreover, Benedictine hospitality, a cornerstone of the Rule, has found renewed significance in modern Church teachings, especially concerning social justice and care for migrants and refugees. The Rule's directive to "welcome all guests as Christ" resonates profoundly in today's context, where the Church is frequently called to act as a refuge for the marginalized and displaced. This Benedictine ideal of hospitality propels the Church's social mission, encouraging parishes and individuals to foster an environment of radical inclusivity, where every person is treated with dignity and respect.

Modern pastoral care also mirrors the Rule's attentiveness to the individual. Benedict's guidelines for abbots to understand the unique needs of each monk underscore the Church's contemporary emphasis on personalized spiritual guidance. In the confessional, in spiritual direction, and in day-to-day parish life, the principles of understanding and individual care prove indispensable. This beneficially shapes the Church's engagement with diverse congregations, helping tailor spiritual and social support to fit varied needs.

The Rule's advocacy for stability and community life challenges modern tendencies toward excessive individualism. In a society where personal autonomy often trumps collective well-being, Benedictine teachings invite a robust re-evaluation. The Church today seeks to bolster community life, urging the faithful to find Christ in one another and to participate actively in communal worship and service. This resonates with the Rule's call for steadfastness within a community, reminding us that we are interwoven into a larger divine narrative.

Furthermore, the Benedictine principle of obedience can be juxtaposed with the Church's understanding of obedience as a loving submission to God's will, rather than a mere hierarchical construct. Within the framework of modern ecclesiology, obedience transforms into a dynamic relationship of trust and mutual growth between the laity and the clergy. The Rule's nuanced vision of obedience – as listening and responding with an open heart – encourages a deeper spiritual maturity that is vital for fostering responsible and engaged discipleship today.

The Rule's liturgical wisdom also proves invaluable in renewing the Church's sacramental life. Its detailed prescriptions for the Divine Office immerse the faithful in a rhythm that sanctifies time itself. By advocating for regular intervals of prayer, the Rule prefigures the Church's call for a renewed liturgical consciousness, wherein every moment can become an encounter with the sacred. This reinstitution of liturgical life complements the Church's call for renewed emphasis on the Eucharist and other sacraments as the source and summit of Christian life.

Benedictine silence and contemplation offer answers to the contemporary quest for interior peace in the midst of external turmoil. The Rule's focus on "quiet" and the deliberate cultivation of inner stillness dovetails with the Church's teachings on the significance of spiritual rest and detachment. Amidst a cacophonous modern landscape, these ancient practices provide a sanctuary where the soul can encounter God without distraction. This focus on contemplative stillness becomes increasingly important as the Church seeks to guide modern Christians toward deeper spiritual encounters.

The imperative of stewardship present in the Rule — exemplified in careful management of the monastery's resources — attunes perfectly with the Church's modern emphasis on environmental responsibility and care for creation. The Rule's ecological wisdom encourages today's faithful to adopt sustainable practices that honor God's creation, thus linking Benedictine values with contemporary environmental ethics as outlined in encyclicals like "Laudato Si'."

Lastly, the Rule's concept of "conversion of life" engages poignantly with the Church's call for ongoing personal and communal renewal. Continuous conversion, a staple of the Rule, echoes the Second Vatican Council's vision for the Church as "semper reformanda" (always reforming). This principle of ongoing transformation challenges the modern Church to remain open to the Spirit's movements, encouraging adaptive faithfulness that remains rooted in tradition while also being responsive to current realities.

In summary, the integration of the Rule of Saint Benedict into modern Church teachings is not merely historical happenstance but a providential convergence. The Rule, with its profound insights into communal living, balanced spirituality, and personal holiness, offers a timeless framework that complements and enriches contemporary Catholic practice and social engagement. By revisiting Benedict's wisdom, the Church gains renewed vigor and clarity in its ongoing mission to embody Christ in a multifaceted world. Such integration underlines the perennial relevance of Benedictine spirituality, ensuring its enduring legacy in guiding the faithful towards a deeper and more harmonious relationship with God, neighbor, and creation.

Chapter 23: Benedictine Influence on Other Religious Orders

Benedictine spirituality, characterized by its balanced focus on prayer, work, and community life, cast a profound influence on numerous religious orders throughout history. Many of these orders, seeking structure and depth in their spiritual practices, adopted and adapted elements of the Rule of Saint Benedict. This cross-pollination led to variations uniquely suited to different charisms and missions but still rooted deeply in Benedictine principles. The Cistercians, for instance, intensified the Rule's ascetic aspects, while the Carthusians focused even more rigorously on solitude and silence. These adaptations demonstrate the Rule's flexibility and timelessness, capable of guiding diverse paths to holiness and enriching the broader tapestry of monastic life. As they embraced these Benedictine precepts, these orders not only found a solid foundation for their endeavors but also contributed to the growing legacy of Saint Benedict, whose influence continues to ripple through the annals of Christian monasticism.

Cross-pollination of Monastic Practices

In the fertile soil of monastic traditions, the Rule of Saint Benedict has taken root and flourished, extending its branches far beyond the Benedictine order. This cross-pollination, much like nature's intermingling of flora, was an inevitable progression driven by the spiritual pursuits common to various religious communities. When examining these cross-currents, we find a symbiotic relationship that offers rich insights into the adaptability and universal appeal of Benedict's principles.

The Cistercians particularly offer a compelling case study in this cross-pollination. Founded in 1098 as a response to what they saw as a relaxed adherence to the Rule of Saint Benedict, the Cistercians brought an ardent rigor to pastoral simplicity and manual labor. They sought a return to the original intent of Benedict's precepts, emphasizing asceticism and self-sufficiency. Despite their unique interpretations, the Cistercians exemplified the enduring adaptability of Benedictine principles, illustrating how a foundation of shared values could give rise to distinct yet related expressions of monastic life.

Similarly, the Carthusians encapsulate another dimension of this cross-pollination. Founded by Saint Bruno in the 11th century, the Carthusians embody a balance between eremitic and cenobitic life, blending communal living with solitary contemplation. The Rule of Saint Benedict, while not adopted in its entirety, influenced their statutes significantly, highlighting the fluidity and relevance of Benedict's wisdom. This confluence underscores how the Rule served as a versatile blueprint, fostering both collective identity and individual spiritual pursuit.

Another testament to the Rule's adaptable nature is evident in the mendicant orders, particularly the Franciscans and Dominicans. Though these orders emerged with distinct charisms and missions, focusing more on itinerant preaching and active ministry than on the cloistered life, they still drew heavily on monastic traditions. The disciplined prayer life, communal living, and vows of poverty within these orders bear the DNA of Benedictine spirituality, albeit expressed through different missions and lifestyles.

Moreover, the Benedictine framework found echoes in the foundations of the Canons Regular of Saint Augustine. These communities, which aimed to combine the clerical life of priests with communal living, leaned heavily on the Benedictine ideals of stability, communal prayer, and pastoral care. Though they anchored themselves primarily in the Augustinian Rule, the symbiotic interweaving of Benedictine principles is unmistakable. This hybridization forms a tapestry of monastic discipline that resonates across various orders, emphasizing a unified quest for divine proximity.

Furthermore, the contemplative orders, such as the Carmelites, demonstrate another layer of this rich interchange. Although they were initially established as a hermitic community on Mount Carmel, the Carmelites later adapted a more communal lifestyle, incrementally influenced by Benedictine and other monastic customs. The integration of structured prayer times, communal activities, and contemplative practices show how Benedict's Rule seeped into their spiritual framework, nurturing a balanced life of action and contemplation.

The feminine monastic engagement with Benedictine traditions also exhibits a profound level of cross-pollination. Orders such as the Poor Clares, founded by Saint Clare of Assisi under the inspiration of Saint Francis, adopted many of the communal and contemplative aspects that were quintessentially Benedictine. Despite their distinct Franciscan identity, the practical applications of communal living and dedication to prayer reflect a shared heritage that broadens the influence of Benedictine spirituality.

Over the centuries, even the more secluded and ascetic branches of monasticism could not escape the far-reaching tendrils of Benedict's ideology. The Camaldolese Hermits, for instance, combined elements of solitary hermitage with cenobitic community life, embodying a duality that Benedict himself might have admired. Their practices, while unique, owe much to the principles of moderation and balance championed in Benedict's Rule.

The proliferation and adaptation of the Rule of Saint Benedict into various reform movements further illustrate this cross-pollination. The Cluniac Reforms of the 10th century sought not just to renew monastic life but also to elevate it through elaborate liturgy and heightened artistic expressions. These reforms, while distinctly Cluniac, were deeply rooted in the Benedictine tradition, demonstrating the resilience and adaptability of the Rule's core values even in an era of transformation and renewal.

Similarly, the later reforms of the Trappists, an offshoot of the Cistercian Order, brought another wave of rigorous observance. Founded in the 17th century, the Trappists embraced silence and manual labor with a fervor that recalls the early days of Benedictine simplicity. This reform movement did not just revive old traditions but infused them with renewed vigor, emphasizing ascetic pastoral practices inherited from their Benedictine predecessors.

The Jesuits, although not traditionally monastic in the same sense as the Benedictines, were nonetheless influenced by the stability and contemplative grounding of monastic life. Their adaptation and integration of these practices into their active, missionary lifestyle highlight how the Benedictine traditions could be refashioned to serve different spiritual and pastoral needs, transcending the boundaries of strictly monastic communities.

Likewise, the cross-pollination extends beyond the confines of Roman Catholic traditions, influencing Eastern Orthodox monasticism. Though the Orthodox Church has its own profound monastic heritage, the spread of Benedictine ideas during times of cultural and religious exchange helped inform some of the organizational and spiritual structures within Eastern monasteries. This intercultural exchange enriches understanding, showing how Benedict's ideals are both universal and adaptable across different theological landscapes.

In essence, the Rule of Saint Benedict acts like a seed that, once planted, grows and branches out in myriad directions. Each religious community and reform movement, while preserving its unique characteristics, carries within it the seminal influence of Benedictine thought. This cross-pollination of monastic practices provides a mosaic of spiritual governance, a testament to the enduring relevance and adaptability of Saint Benedict's wisdom.

The resonance of Benedictine principles across various monastic and religious traditions is a testament to their universal applicability. They offer a common ground upon which different orders can build their unique spiritual edifices while maintaining a connectedness to the foundational values of prayer, community, and balance. This enduring influence not only enriches the orders themselves but also offers a cohesive spiritual heritage that continues to inspire and guide faithful across diverse traditions.

Chapter 24: Reflections on the Rule

In contemplating the perennial wisdom encapsulated in Saint Benedict's Rule, one finds a mirror reflecting the soul's ardent yearning for divine order amidst a chaotic world. This sacred legacy shines forth not merely as an antiquated text but as a living testament to the transformative power of disciplined spiritual practice. Stories abound of contemporary lives—both lay and cleric—reshaped by the Rule's enduring precepts of humility, stability, and obedience. One can envisage a tapestry woven with threads of personal testimonies, each narrative a testament to the Rule's adaptability to modern exigencies. Whether in bustling cities or secluded monasteries, Benedict's principles resonate, guiding souls toward a harmonious existence that transcends temporal bounds, illuminating the path to a sanctified communal life that honors both individual growth and collective well-being.

Personal Stories and Testimonies

Within the hushed confines of monasteries and the bustling turmoil of the secular world, the Rule of Saint Benedict has left an indelible mark on countless lives. Monks and nuns, guided by its precepts, recount tales of spiritual awakening and communal harmony, testifying to the transformative power of Benedictine principles. For them, the Rule is not just a set of regulations but a living, breathing guide that shapes their daily existence—a source of solace during tribulations and a beacon of light in moments of doubt. Lay associates and modern-day oblates find in its timeless wisdom a pathway to balance work, prayer, and community, integrating age-old teachings into the fabric of contemporary life. These personal stories illuminate the enduring appeal of the Rule, demonstrating its ability to mold lives filled with purpose, resilience, and grace, transcending centuries and cultural divides.

Modern Lives Shaped by Benedictine Principles are veritable testimonies to the enduring character of Saint Benedict's timeless wisdom. Stretching from the cloisters into bustling urban landscapes, his Rule has transcended the venerable walls of medieval monasteries, touching the pulses of contemporary life. Within this labyrinth of daily existence, embedded principles such as balance, community, and humility often serve as guiding lights, illuminating pathways for both the devout and those tangentially connected to the faith.

Take, for instance, the principle of *ora et labora*, or "pray and work." The synthesis of spiritual and manual labor set forth by Saint Benedict finds fertile ground not just in monastic settings but in homes, schools, and corporate offices. Balances struck between contemplation and activity, sacred and mundane, are evident when individuals punctuate their hectic schedules with moments of quiet or prayer. Embodying this balance seems kin to weaving a delicate tapestry where threads of divine consideration interlace with the fabric of daily tasks.

The principle of hospitality, another cornerstone of the Benedictine Rule, remains vividly relevant in an era marked by disconnection and individualism. This directive to treat every guest as Christ reverberates through acts of kindness and inclusivity in modern settings. Whether it be a simple act of sharing a meal or extending emotional support to a stranger or colleague, hospitality speaks to the core of human dignity and interdependence.

Moreover, the cultivation of community life, intricately detailed by Saint Benedict, finds echoes in the modern pursuit of creating supportive and interconnected environments. Just as monks leaned on one another, today's society sees the value in constructing networks of empathy and mutual aid. From community service projects to neighborhood initiatives, individuals are translating monastic ideals into systemic actions that uplift collective well-being.

Humility, the bedrock of the Benedictine ethic, presents a profound counter-narrative to the prevailing culture of self-promotion and materialism. The virtue of recognizing one's limitations and the grace in service to others provides a reprieve from egoistic drives and fosters a spirit of genuine humanness and compassion. In workplaces and homes, this humility cultivates a respectful and cooperative ethos, one that is desperately needed in a hyper-competitive world.

It's also worth noting the rise of Benedictine Oblates, laypeople who choose to live according to the Benedictine Rule while remaining in their secular vocations. Their lives are emblematic of how these ancient principles can be harmonized with modern responsibilities. They participate in communal prayers, engage in charitable activities, and even adapt the Rule's precepts into their professional conduct, thereby creating a seamless blend of monastic and secular life.

Teaching and education reflect yet another domain where Benedictine principles subtly imbue modern practices. Educators incorporating a Benedictine approach often emphasize the holistic development of students—intellectual growth coupled with moral and spiritual education. This integration of head and heart stands in sharp contrast to a purely utilitarian education model, fostering well-rounded human beings rather than mere career professionals.

The emphasis on stability, a value profoundly articulated in the Rule, offers a lens through which one can reimagine contemporary notions of commitment and rootedness. In a world characterized by rapid change and fleeting allegiances, the call to stability urges us to anchor ourselves, whether in familial bonds, careers, or communities. This stability engenders resilience, providing a firm foundation amidst life's uncertainties.

Benedictine ideals also influence modern social justice movements. The commitment to charity, care for the marginalized, and a life of simplicity presents an ethical framework for advocating against social inequalities and environmental degradation. The emphasis on communal living and shared resources offers a blueprint for sustainable practices, both ecologically and economically, thus serving as a moral compass for addressing contemporary crises.

Thus, the symbiotic relationship between Benedictine principles and modern life creates a fertile ground for spiritual and ethical rejuvenation. It is a compelling tapestry where ancient wisdom threads through the fabric of modernity, enriching lives and sustaining communities. Weaving these principles into our everyday existence, we find ourselves not just echoing the Benedictine spirit but embodying its transformative power in our very being. In doing so, the timeless dance between ora et labora, the heartbeat of community, and the quiet grace of humility continues to play out, shaping modern lives with the wisdom of centuries past.

Chapter 25: Future Directions for Benedictine Living

As we forge ahead into the 21st century, the Benedictine way of life beckons with timeless relevance and modern adaptability. The balance of ora et labora (prayer and work) continues to offer a roadmap for a harmonious existence in an increasingly dissonant world. Embracing innovative means to foster community, monastic traditions may find new expression through digital monasteries, while maintaining the steadfast commitment to manual labor and scholarly pursuits. The environmental consciousness burgeoning in our age aligns seamlessly with Benedictine stewardship, calling for a deeper symbiosis with nature. Ancient wisdom thus intertwines with contemporary challenges, inviting a fresh yet rooted perspective that upholds the enduring legacy of Saints Benedict and Scholastica. In this evolving landscape, the Benedictine ethos serves as a beacon, guiding both monastics and laypersons toward spiritual and communal flourishing.

Adaptation and Growth in the 21st Century

As we examine Benedictine living in the modern era, it becomes evident that the principles laid out by Saints Benedict and Scholastica are more vital than ever. The world today faces unprecedented challenges—social instability, environmental crises, and a pervasive sense of existential angst. Amidst this volatility, the Benedictine way offers a sanctuary of stability and purpose. Its very essence—rooted in prayer, work, and community—is a countercultural manifesto that addresses the deep-seated longing for meaning in contemporary society.

In this century, technology and globalization have drastically transformed human life. While these advancements bring numerous benefits, they also foster isolation and superficial connections. The Benedictine model of communal living presents an antidote to this fragmentation. Modern Benedictine monasteries, equipped with the same timeless Rule but adapted for today's context, become havens for those seeking genuine human interaction and spiritual depth.

At the core of this adaptation is the principle of "ora et labora"—prayer and work. These twin pillars remain as relevant today as they were in the sixth century. However, the nature of work has expanded. Beyond manual labor, today's Benedictines engage in intellectual, technological, and environmental endeavors. In an age overly reliant on digital distractions, the disciplined rhythm of the Benedictine daily life offers a grounded alternative. By integrating traditional practices with contemporary skills, they bridge the ancient with the modern, creating a holistic approach to life's multifaceted demands.

The role of education is another significant aspect of Benedictine adaptation. Historically, monasteries were centers of learning, preserving and disseminating knowledge through the ages. Today, this legacy continues through modern monastic schools and institutions. They provide environments where students receive not only excellent education but also moral and spiritual formation. This integration of knowledge and values equips young minds to navigate a world rife with ethical ambiguities.

Moreover, Benedictine spirituality has found fertile ground beyond the cloister walls. The rise of Benedictine Oblates and lay associates exemplifies this expansion. These individuals, though living outside the monastery, commit to embodying Benedictine values in their daily lives. This movement reflects a thirst for spiritual depth in secular life, illustrating how the Rule's wisdom extends its reach to all corners of society.

Furthermore, the impact of Benedictine practices on ecological consciousness is noteworthy. With a heritage deeply connected to the land, modern Benedictines are at the forefront of sustainable living. They advocate for environmental stewardship, understanding that caring for creation is a divine mandate. Through organic farming, renewable energy initiatives, and environmental education, they model a harmonious relationship with nature, inspiring others to follow suit.

The 21st century also witnesses an increasing dialogue between faiths. The ecumenical and interfaith engagements of modern Benedictines reflect their commitment to peace and understanding. By fostering dialogues and collaborative efforts, they build bridges in a fragmented world. This openness to diverse perspectives enriches their own spiritual practice, making Benedictine spirituality a living, evolving tradition.

Challenges certainly abound. Secularism, dwindling vocations, and the demands of modern life pose significant hurdles. However, these challenges also present opportunities for growth. Innovative approaches to monastic living, including virtual communities and digital evangelism, show how Benedictines are adapting to maintain their spiritual vigor. The resilience of the Benedictine spirit lies in its capacity to innovate without losing sight of foundational principles.

In sum, the path forward for Benedictine living in the 21st century is one of dynamic balance—holding fast to ancient wisdom while embracing contemporary realities. The adaptability of the Benedictine way, with its emphasis on stability, humility, and stewardship, provides a powerful counter-narrative to the ephemeral nature of modern existence. As we navigate this century's complexities, the enduring legacy of Saints Benedict and Scholastica offers a beacon of hope, guiding us towards a more integrated, harmonious life.

The resurgence of Benedictine principles in various sectors highlights their universal applicability. In the corporate world, for instance, Benedictine leadership models are gaining traction. The emphasis on servant leadership, community, and ethical integrity resonates deeply with modern organizational needs. Companies increasingly seek to align their practices with these values, fostering workplaces that prioritize human well-being over mere profit.

Healthcare is another domain where Benedictine values are making a significant impact. In an industry often criticized for its impersonal nature, the Benedictine approach to care—characterized by compassion, humility, and holistic attention—offers a transformative alternative. Hospitals and care facilities inspired by Benedictine principles focus on the dignity and spiritual needs of patients, promoting a more humane and compassionate healthcare system.

Additionally, the arts and culture sector is experiencing a Benedictine revival. Monastic communities have always been patrons of the arts, and this tradition continues today. Through music, visual arts, and literature, modern Benedictines contribute to the cultural tapestry, creating works that reflect their spiritual insights and ethical commitments. These artistic endeavors serve as a medium for contemplation and spiritual reflection, enriching both the creators and the audience.

In the realm of social justice, Benedictine communities are actively engaged in advocacy and outreach. They work tirelessly to address issues such as poverty, inequality, and human rights. Rooted in the principle of hospitality, Benedictines extend their resources and compassion to marginalized individuals and communities. Their social initiatives embody the Gospel's call to serve "the least of these," offering tangible expressions of love and justice in a broken world.

Lastly, the personal transformation experienced by individuals who embrace Benedictine spirituality is profound. Testimonials abound of people finding renewed purpose, inner peace, and a sense of belonging through adherence to the Rule. These personal stories underscore the timeless relevance of Benedictine principles, affirming their power to shape lives in meaningful and lasting ways.

As we move further into the 21st century, the adaptability of Benedictine living remains its greatest strength. The ability to apply ancient wisdom to contemporary challenges ensures its continued relevance. By fostering communities rooted in prayer, work, and mutual support, Benedictines contribute to a more compassionate and just world. Their enduring legacy, grounded in the teachings of Saints Benedict and Scholastica, continues to inspire and guide individuals and societies towards greater spiritual and ethical growth.

In conclusion, the journey of Benedictine living in the 21st century is one of profound adaptation and growth. The sacred rhythm of communal life, the integration of traditional and modern practices, and the commitment to education, environmental stewardship, and social justice—all these elements converge to form a vibrant and dynamic expression of Benedictine spirituality. As we face the uncertainties and complexities of this era, the wisdom of Saints Benedict and Scholastica stands as a steadfast beacon, guiding us towards a future illuminated by faith, hope, and love.

Conclusion

The inquiry into the lives and impacts of Saints Benedict and Scholastica brings us face to face with not just the two towering figures of early Christian monasticism, but with a set of ideals that have persisted through the corridors of time. Through our exploration, we've tread the rugged paths of ancient monastic life, observed the disciplined routines of holy men and women, and witnessed the ripples of their influence spreading across centuries and continents.

Saint Benedict's life exhibits a scenery of both adversity and divine purpose. His establishment of Monte Cassino stands as an architectural and spiritual monument to Christian perseverance. In a world increasingly distant from the chaos and uncertainties of early medieval Europe, the relevance of Benedict's Rule cannot be overstated. It offers a framework of humility, stability, and obedience—principles that transcend the walls of monastic settings to provide valuable guidance even today.

Contrasting this robust foundation, Saint Scholastica complements her brother's stern ethos with a spirit of nurturing and loving devotion. Her relationship with Saint Benedict exemplifies how familial bonds can embody deeper spiritual truths, integrating the masculine and feminine dimensions of spiritual life into a harmonious whole. Their intertwined lives narrate a tale of mutual dependence, where the rigorous meets the tender, and discipline coalesces with love.

In the labyrinth of gender roles within Benedictine monasticism, Scholastica emerges as a beacon, illuminating the significant yet often understated role of women. Through her influence, we uncover how gendered lenses can obscure the full spectrum of spiritual and communal life, subsequently broadening our understanding of early Christian communities.

Benedictine spirituality emphasizes not just prayer and contemplation but also the sanctity of labor. This melding of spiritual and physical endeavors challenges any dichotomy between the sacred and the mundane. Through agriculture, artisanal crafts, and scholarly pursuits, Benedictines have perpetuated the belief that work—in all its forms—is imbued with spiritual significance. Each effort, no matter how trivial it may seem, is performed as an offering to the divine.

A pivotal aspect of Benedictine life is its dedication to the preservation of knowledge. Monastic schools and scriptoria stand behind the veil of history as silent guardians of human intellect. The meticulous copying and preserving of manuscripts have ensured that wisdom traverses generations, enlightening both the cloistered and the layman alike. In contemporary times, this dedication continues to resonate in the educational institutions founded by Benedictines worldwide.

The societal engagement of Benedictine monks and nuns transcends their cloistered existence. By extending charity and care for the poor and sick, they manifest the values they cherish. Their outreach efforts personify the principles of Saint Benedict's Rule, bridging spiritual aspirations with tangible acts of kindness. This symbiosis with society at large has made monasteries pivotal in the cultural and intellectual maturation of local communities and beyond.

As these practices disseminated across medieval Europe, they sparked the establishment of monasteries far and wide. This expansion speaks to the Rule's adaptability, echoing its principles across diverse cultures and communities. Whether through Cluniac reforms or other religious movements, the evolution of Benedictine ideals demonstrates a dynamic tradition, continually reinterpreted to meet the exigencies of the times.

Modern interpretations of the Rule underscore its enduring applicability. Amid present-day challenges, the Rule serves as a spiritual compass, guiding individuals and communities alike. Oblates and lay associates today reflect the Rule's inclusive nature, embedding its precepts into their daily lives and offering a testament to its cross-generational appeal.

Contemporary monastic communities wrestle with both challenges and opportunities. The 21st century demands an astute balance of adaptation and preservation, where ancient wisdom meets modern exigencies. Through dialogues, ecumenical engagements, and an unwavering commitment to spiritual and communal life, Benedictine spirituality continues to evolve, offering a sanctuary of stability in a rapidly changing world.

Thus, the legacy of Saints Benedict and Scholastica is one of enduring relevance. They crafted a vision of a utopian community grounded in the real, tangible world—a vision that navigates through the labyrinths of time, continually redefining itself yet remaining anchored in its core principles. Their lives prompt us to reflect upon our paths, urging us to weave prayer, work, and community into the fabric of our everyday existence.

The pilgrimage and veneration of these saints underscore their monumental influence. Sites like Monte Cassino serve as spiritual epicenters, drawing pilgrims and testament to the profound impact of their lives. These places not only honor their legacies but also inspire modern visitors towards deeper spiritual reflection and renewal.

The contributions of Benedictines to Western culture and education reflect an invaluable intellectual heritage. From universities to social justice endeavors, their influence has embedded itself in the very tapestry of society. These enduring contributions underscore the dynamic and transformative power of the Benedictine way of life over centuries.

In reflecting upon the principles of the Rule through personal stories and testimonies, we find modern lives profoundly shaped by these ancient precepts. This collection of lived experiences brings to light the Rule's capacity to instigate meaningful transformation within individuals and communities, navigating the ebb and flow of life's vicissitudes.

The future directions for Benedictine living suggest a landscape ripe for growth and adaptation. The core principles remain as steadfast anchors, while innovation and interpretation forge pathways for relevance in contemporary times. It's a journey of steadfast perseverance and inspired renewal, embodying the timeless essence of Benedictine spirituality.

In summation, as we conclude our exploration, it is evident that Saints Benedict and Scholastica left an indelible imprint on the spiritual and cultural fabric of their world—a legacy that flows seamlessly into ours. Their lives and ideals veil us in a rich mosaic of faith, labor, and devotion—a living tradition that fuels our quest for a balanced, meaningful existence. Their luminescence guides us still, through the alleys of our own spiritual and temporal journeys, calling us to integrate the sacred and the everyday with uncompromised fervor.

Appendix A: Resources for Further Study

Embarking on a journey through the annals of Benedictine monasticism and the lives of Saints Benedict and Scholastica offers profound insights. For those who wish to delve deeper into the philosophical, theological, and historical dimensions of this rich tradition, a comprehensive list of resources is indispensable. Below, you'll find selected works that provide a broader understanding of the subject matter discussed in this volume.

Primary Sources

- **The Rule of Saint Benedict**: The foundational text for Benedictine monasticism. It provides guidelines on communal living, work, and spiritual practice.

- **Dialogues** by Pope Gregory the Great: A significant source for understanding the lives of early monastics, including Benedict and Scholastica.

Historical Context

- **The Benedictines in the Middle Ages** by James G. Clark: This book explores the historical evolution of Benedictine monasticism throughout Medieval Europe.

- **Saint Benedict: Father of Western Monasticism** by Julian Stead: A detailed biography of Saint Benedict, offering insights into his life and legacy.

Spiritual and Theological Reflections

- **Monastic Practices** by Charles Cummings: An insightful guide into the spiritual practices of monastic life, closely aligned with the Rule of Saint Benedict.

- **The Benedictine Handbook** by The Liturgical Press: A comprehensive guide that includes commentaries on the Rule, prayers, and practical advice for adopting Benedictine principles.

Gender Studies in Monastic Life

- **Sisters in Arms: Catholic Nuns Through Two Millennia** by Jo Ann Kay McNamara: A thorough exploration of the role of women in the Church, including figures like Saint Scholastica.

- **The Forgotten Desert Mothers: Sayings, Lives, and Stories of Early Christian Women** by Laura Swan: Although broader in scope, this book provides valuable context on the roles of women in early Christian monastic communities.

Cultural and Social Impact

- **The Benedictine Tradition** by Columba Stewart: Offers a panoramic view of the influence of Benedictine monks and nuns on Western culture and intellectual thought.

- **Work and Pray: Living the Benedictine Way** by Columba Stewart: This book distills the wisdom of the Benedictine tradition into practical guidance for contemporary life.

Modern Adaptations

- **Seeking God: The Way of Saint Benedict** by Esther de Waal: A modern reflection on how the Rule of Saint Benedict can inform contemporary spiritual practices.

- **Always We Begin Again: The Benedictine Way of Living** by John McQuiston II: A contemporary interpretation of the Rule, emphasizing its relevance in today's world.

These resources provide a scaffold upon which further knowledge and deeper contemplation can be built. Through these works, one can traverse the intricate paths of monastic thought and practice, ever enriched by the steadfast examples of Saints Benedict and Scholastica.

Quotations and applications

1. "Prayer is the key that unlocks the door to communion with God, for in prayer, we open our hearts and invite His presence."

2. "Humility is the foundation upon which true holiness is built, for it is through humility that we recognize our need for God's grace."

3. "Obedience to God's will is the surest path to freedom and peace, for in surrendering our own desires, we find true fulfillment."

4 "Penance is not a burden to be endured, but a gift to be embraced, for through penance, we are purified and draw closer to God's mercy."

5. "Charity is the language of love spoken through our actions, for in serving others, we reflect the selfless love of Christ."

6. "Ora et labora, pray and work, for in the balance of contemplation and action, we find harmony and fulfillment."

7. "The Holy Eucharist is the source and summit of our faith, for in receiving the Body and Blood of Christ, we are nourished and united with Him."

8. "The sacraments are sacred encounters with God's grace, through which we are transformed and drawn deeper into His love."

9. "Prayer is not a monologue, but a dialogue with God, for in listening to His voice, we find guidance and peace."

10. "True humility is not thinking less of ourselves, but thinking of ourselves less, directing our thoughts and actions towards God and others."

"Prayer is the key that unlocks the door to communion with God, for in prayer, we open our hearts and invite His presence."

Application: Saint Scholastica's life was deeply rooted in prayer, as seen in her annual meetings with her brother Saint Benedict. During their last meeting, her fervent prayer for continued spiritual conversation with Saint Benedict led to a miraculous storm, illustrating her deep communion with God and the power of her prayer.

"Humility is the foundation upon which true holiness is built, for it is through humility that we recognize our need for God's grace."

Application: Saint Scholastica's humility was evident in her leadership of her community of nuns. She recognized her need for God's grace and guided her sisters with a humble heart, fostering a spirit of humility and holiness within the convent.

"Obedience to God's will is the surest path to freedom and peace, for in surrendering our own desires, we find true fulfillment."

Application: Saint Scholastica's life was a testament to her obedience to God's will. By following the monastic path and adhering to the Rule of Saint Benedict, she found peace and fulfillment, and her leadership inspired her nuns to do the same.

"Penance is not a burden to be endured, but a gift to be embraced, for through penance, we are purified and draw closer to God's mercy."

Application: Saint Scholastica embraced penance as a means of spiritual purification. She taught her nuns to see penance as a gift, helping them to draw closer to God's mercy and grow in holiness.

"Charity is the language of love spoken through our actions, for in serving others, we reflect the selfless love of Christ."

Application: Saint Scholastica's life was marked by acts of charity and service. She taught her nuns to serve others selflessly, reflecting the love of Christ in their actions and fostering a community rooted in love and compassion.

"Ora et labora, pray and work, for in the balance of contemplation and action, we find harmony and fulfillment."

Application: Saint Scholastica adhered to the Saint Benedictine motto of "ora et labora" (pray and work). She balanced her life of prayer and contemplation with practical work, finding harmony and fulfillment in this rhythm and instilling this balance in her community.

"The Holy Eucharist is the source and summit of our faith, for in receiving the Body and Blood of Christ, we are nourished and united with Him."

Application: The Eucharist was central to Saint Scholastica's spiritual life. By receiving the Body and Blood of Christ, she and her nuns were spiritually nourished and united with Him, which was crucial for their spiritual growth and community life.

"The sacraments are sacred encounters with God's grace, through which we are transformed and drawn deeper into His love."

Application: Saint Scholastica valued the sacraments as vital encounters with God's grace. These sacraments, especially the Eucharist and confession, were transformative, drawing her and her community deeper into God's love.

"Prayer is not a monologue, but a dialogue with God, for in listening to His voice, we find guidance and peace."

Application: Saint Scholastica understood prayer as a dialogue with God. Her life of deep prayer and contemplation allowed her to listen to God's voice, finding guidance and peace, which she imparted to her nuns.

"True humility is not thinking less of ourselves, but thinking of ourselves less, directing our thoughts and actions towards God and others."

Application: Saint Scholastica's humility was demonstrated by her selfless focus on God and her community. She thought of herself less and directed her thoughts and actions towards serving God and others, exemplifying true humility and inspiring her nuns to do the same.

These applications show how the principles in these quotes were lived out in the life and teachings of Saint Scholastica, deeply influencing her spirituality and the community she led.

11. "In obedience, we surrender our will to God's, trusting that His plans are greater than our own."

12. "Penance is a sacred journey of self-reflection and repentance, drawing us closer to God's mercy and forgiveness."

13. "Charity is the outward expression of the love that dwells within us, a selfless act of kindness towards others."

14. "Work becomes a prayer when we offer it to God, for in our labor, we glorify His name."

15. "The Holy Eucharist is the gift of Christ's presence among us, a sacred mystery that nourishes our souls."

16. "The sacraments are channels of God's grace, tangible signs of His love and mercy in our lives."

17. "Prayer is the anchor that grounds us amidst life's storms, a lifeline connecting us to God's presence and guidance."

18. "Humility is the recognition of our dependence on God, acknowledging that He is the source of all that is good."

19. "Obedience is the path of trust, surrendering our own will to God's wisdom and guidance."

20. "Penance is an act of love, a willingness to make amends and seek reconciliation with God and others."

"In obedience, we surrender our will to God's, trusting that His plans are greater than our own."

Application: Saint Benedict's Rule emphasizes the importance of obedience to God and to the abbot as a means of spiritual growth. By surrendering personal will and trusting in God's greater plans, Saint Benedictine monks learn humility and discipline, essential for their spiritual journey.

"Penance is a sacred journey of self-reflection and repentance, drawing us closer to God's mercy and forgiveness."

Application: Penance is integral to Saint Benedictine spirituality. Saint Benedict taught his monks to embrace penance as a means of self-reflection and repentance, leading them closer to God's mercy and forgiveness. This practice helps monks to purify their hearts and souls.

"Charity is the outward expression of the love that dwells within us, a selfless act of kindness towards others."

Application: Charity is a core principle in the Rule of Saint Benedict. Saint Benedict instructed his monks to practice hospitality and care for the poor and strangers, reflecting the love of Christ through their selfless acts of kindness.

"Work becomes a prayer when we offer it to God, for in our labor, we glorify His name."

Application: The Saint Benedictine motto "ora et labora" (pray and work) embodies this quote. Saint Benedict taught that all labor, when offered to God, becomes a form of prayer. This sanctifies daily work and glorifies God's name through diligent and faithful labor.

"The Holy Eucharist is the gift of Christ's presence among us, a sacred mystery that nourishes our souls."

Application: The Eucharist was central to the spiritual life in Saint Benedictine monasteries. Saint Benedict recognized it as a sacred mystery that nourishes the soul and unites the monks with Christ, providing spiritual strength and grace.

"The sacraments are channels of God's grace, tangible signs of His love and mercy in our lives."

Application: Saint Benedict valued the sacraments as essential encounters with God's grace. Through the sacraments, particularly the Eucharist and confession, monks receive tangible signs of God's love and mercy, which are crucial for their spiritual growth.

"Prayer is the anchor that grounds us amidst life's storms, a lifeline connecting us to God's presence and guidance."

Application: Prayer was the cornerstone of Saint Benedict's Rule. He structured the monastic day around the Liturgy of the Hours, ensuring that prayer anchored the monks' lives, connecting them to God's presence and guidance amidst all challenges.

"Humility is the recognition of our dependence on God, acknowledging that He is the source of all that is good."

Application: Humility is a foundational virtue in Saint Benedictine spirituality. Saint Benedict taught that recognizing one's dependence on God is essential for true holiness. This acknowledgment fosters a spirit of humility, where all good is seen as coming from God.

"Obedience is the path of trust, surrendering our own will to God's wisdom and guidance."

Application: Obedience to the abbot and the Rule is central in Saint Benedictine life. Saint Benedict believed that by surrendering their own will, monks learn to trust in God's wisdom and guidance, which leads to spiritual growth and community harmony.

"Penance is an act of love, a willingness to make amends and seek reconciliation with God and others."

Application: Saint Benedict viewed penance as an act of love. It involves making amends and seeking reconciliation with God and the community. This practice not only purifies the individual but also strengthens communal bonds, reflecting the love of Christ.

These applications highlight how the principles in these quotes were lived out in the life and teachings of Saint Benedict, deeply influencing Saint Benedictine spirituality and monastic practices.

11. "In obedience, we surrender our will to God's, trusting that His plans are greater than our own."

12. "Penance is a sacred journey of self-reflection and repentance, drawing us closer to God's mercy and forgiveness."

13. "Charity is the outward expression of the love that dwells within us, a selfless act of kindness towards others."

14. "Work becomes a prayer when we offer it to God, for in our labor, we glorify His name."

15. "The Holy Eucharist is the gift of Christ's presence among us, a sacred mystery that nourishes our souls."

16. "The sacraments are channels of God's grace, tangible signs of His love and mercy in our lives."

17. "Prayer is the anchor that grounds us amidst life's storms, a lifeline connecting us to God's presence and guidance."

18. "Humility is the recognition of our dependence on God, acknowledging that He is the source of all that is good."

19. "Obedience is the path of trust, surrendering our own will to God's wisdom and guidance."

20. "Penance is an act of love, a willingness to make amends and seek reconciliation with God and others."

"In obedience, we surrender our will to God's, trusting that His plans are greater than our own."

Application: Saint Scholastica exemplified obedience by embracing her vocation as a nun and following the Rule of Saint Benedict faithfully. By surrendering her will to God's, she trusted in His plans, leading her to a life of holiness and service.

"Penance is a sacred journey of self-reflection and repentance, drawing us closer to God's mercy and forgiveness."

Application: Saint Scholastica practiced penance as a means of spiritual growth and reconciliation with God. Through self-reflection and repentance, she drew closer to God's mercy and forgiveness, exemplifying humility and contrition.

"Charity is the outward expression of the love that dwells within us, a selfless act of kindness towards others."

Application: Saint Scholastica lived a life of charity, showing kindness and compassion towards others, especially her fellow nuns. Her selfless acts of love reflected the love of Christ dwelling within her, fostering unity and community within the convent.

"Work becomes a prayer when we offer it to God, for in our labor, we glorify His name."

Application: Saint Scholastica viewed her daily tasks and responsibilities within the convent as opportunities to glorify God. By offering her work to Him, she transformed her labor into a form of prayer, seeking to honor and glorify God in all she did.

"The Holy Eucharist is the gift of Christ's presence among us, a sacred mystery that nourishes our souls."

Application: Saint Scholastica cherished the Eucharist as the source of spiritual nourishment and communion with Christ. She participated devoutly in the Eucharistic liturgy, recognizing it as a sacred mystery that nourished her soul and strengthened her faith.

"The sacraments are channels of God's grace, tangible signs of His love and mercy in our lives."

Application: Saint Scholastica valued the sacraments as means of encountering God's grace and love. Through the sacraments, especially confession and the Eucharist, she experienced God's mercy and forgiveness, deepening her relationship with Him.

"Prayer is the anchor that grounds us amidst life's storms, a lifeline connecting us to God's presence and guidance."

Application: Saint Scholastica's life was rooted in prayer, which provided her with strength and guidance, especially during times of difficulty. Prayer served as her anchor amidst life's storms, connecting her to God's presence and providing her with guidance and peace.

"Humility is the recognition of our dependence on God, acknowledging that He is the source of all that is good."

Application: Saint Scholastica embodied humility by recognizing her dependence on God for all things. She acknowledged that He was the source of all that is good and lived her life in humble submission to His will, trusting in His wisdom and providence.

"Obedience is the path of trust, surrendering our own will to God's wisdom and guidance."

Application: Saint Scholastica practiced obedience by faithfully following the Rule of Saint Benedict and submitting herself to the authority of her abbess. Through obedience, she trusted in God's wisdom and guidance, surrendering her own will to His divine providence.

"Penance is an act of love, a willingness to make amends and seek reconciliation with God and others."

Application: Saint Scholastica embraced penance as an act of love and reconciliation with God and others. She willingly sought to make amends for her faults and shortcomings, seeking reconciliation and peace with God and her community.

These applications highlight how the principles in these quotes were lived out in the life and teachings of Saint Scholastica, deeply influencing her spirituality and the community she led.

21. "Charity is a flame that ignites the darkness, spreading warmth and compassion to those in need."

22. "Ora et labora, the rhythm of prayer and work, harmonizing our spiritual and earthly responsibilities."

23. "The Holy Eucharist is a sacred banquet, where we are nourished by the very body and blood of Christ."

24. "The sacraments are encounters with the divine, where God's grace flows abundantly into our lives."

25. "Prayer is the breath of the soul, a constant conversation with God that sustains and uplifts us."

26. "Humility is not weakness, but strength in surrendering our own ego for the sake of God's glory."

27. "Obedience is the path to true freedom, as we align our will with God's perfect plan for our lives."

28. "Penance is a humble response to our shortcomings, a way to grow closer to God and seek His forgiveness."

29. "Charity is the fragrance of Christ, permeating our actions and drawing others closer to His love."

30. "Ora et labora, the sacred dance of prayer and work, where we find God's presence in every moment."

"Charity is a flame that ignites the darkness, spreading warmth and compassion to those in need."

Application: Saint Benedict's life exemplified charity through his hospitality and care for others. His monasteries provided refuge and assistance to travelers, the sick, and the needy, spreading warmth and compassion in a world often plagued by darkness.

"Ora et labora, the rhythm of prayer and work, harmonizing our spiritual and earthly responsibilities."

Application: Saint Benedict embraced the motto "ora et labora" (pray and work) as the foundation of monastic life. He balanced prayer with manual labor, recognizing the importance of both spiritual and earthly responsibilities in achieving harmony and holiness.

"The Holy Eucharist is a sacred banquet, where we are nourished by the very body and blood of Christ."

Application: Saint Benedict revered the Eucharist as the source of spiritual nourishment for his monks. He ensured that the celebration of the Eucharist was central to the monastic day, recognizing it as a sacred banquet where monks were nourished by the body and blood of Christ.

"The sacraments are encounters with the divine, where God's grace flows abundantly into our lives."

Application: Saint Benedict valued the sacraments as channels of God's grace. He encouraged his monks to participate devoutly in the sacraments, recognizing them as encounters with the divine where God's grace flowed abundantly into their lives, strengthening their faith and spiritual growth.

"Prayer is the breath of the soul, a constant conversation with God that sustains and uplifts us."

Application: Saint Benedict prioritized prayer as the foundation of monastic life. He structured the monastic day around the Liturgy of the Hours, ensuring that prayer was a constant conversation with God that sustained and uplifted the souls of his monks.

"Humility is not weakness, but strength in surrendering our own ego for the sake of God's glory."

Application: Saint Benedict embodied humility in his life and teachings. He recognized that true humility was not weakness but strength in surrendering one's own ego for the sake of God's glory. His Rule emphasized humility as essential for spiritual growth and community life.

"Obedience is the path to true freedom, as we align our will with God's perfect plan for our lives."

Application: Saint Benedict emphasized obedience as essential for monastic life. He taught that by aligning their will with God's perfect plan through obedience to the Rule and the abbot, monks found true freedom and fulfillment in their vocation.

"Penance is a humble response to our shortcomings, a way to grow closer to God and seek His forgiveness."

Application: Saint Benedict viewed penance as a means of spiritual growth and reconciliation with God. He encouraged his monks to humbly acknowledge their shortcomings and seek forgiveness through acts of penance, fostering a spirit of contrition and renewal.

"Charity is the fragrance of Christ, permeating our actions and drawing others closer to His love."

Application: Saint Benedict's life was characterized by charity, which he saw as a reflection of Christ's love. His hospitality and care for others permeated his actions, drawing others closer to Christ's love and inspiring them to follow His example.

"Ora et labora, the sacred dance of prayer and work, where we find God's presence in every moment."

Application: Saint Benedict embraced "ora et labora" (pray and work) as a sacred rhythm of monastic life. He saw prayer and work as a sacred dance where God's presence could be found in every moment, leading to a deeper union with Him and spiritual fulfillment.

These applications demonstrate how the principles in these quotes were lived out in the life and teachings of Saint Benedict, profoundly influencing Saint Benedictine spirituality and monastic practices.

21. "Charity is a flame that ignites the darkness, spreading warmth and compassion to those in need."

22. "Ora et labora, the rhythm of prayer and work, harmonizing our spiritual and earthly responsibilities."

23. "The Holy Eucharist is a sacred banquet, where we are nourished by the very body and blood of Christ."

24. "The sacraments are encounters with the divine, where God's grace flows abundantly into our lives."

25. "Prayer is the breath of the soul, a constant conversation with God that sustains and uplifts us."

26. "Humility is not weakness, but strength in surrendering our own ego for the sake of God's glory."

27. "Obedience is the path to true freedom, as we align our will with God's perfect plan for our lives."

28. "Penance is a humble response to our shortcomings, a way to grow closer to God and seek His forgiveness."

29. "Charity is the fragrance of Christ, permeating our actions and drawing others closer to His love."

30. "Ora et labora, the sacred dance of prayer and work, where we find God's presence in every moment."

"Charity is a flame that ignites the darkness, spreading warmth and compassion to those in need."

Application: Saint Scholastica's life was marked by charity and compassion. She dedicated herself to serving others, especially the poor and marginalized, spreading warmth and compassion to those in need through her acts of kindness and generosity.

"Ora et labora, the rhythm of prayer and work, harmonizing our spiritual and earthly responsibilities."

Application: Saint Scholastica embraced the Saint Benedictine motto "ora et labora" (pray and work) in her life as a nun. She balanced her life of prayer with practical work, recognizing the importance of harmonizing spiritual and earthly responsibilities in her pursuit of holiness.

"The Holy Eucharist is a sacred banquet, where we are nourished by the very body and blood of Christ."

Application: Saint Scholastica held the Eucharist in deep reverence. She participated devoutly in the Eucharistic liturgy, recognizing it as a sacred banquet where she was nourished by the very body and blood of Christ, drawing strength and grace from this sacramental encounter.

"The sacraments are encounters with the divine, where God's grace flows abundantly into our lives."

Application: Saint Scholastica cherished the sacraments as encounters with the divine. She participated fervently in the sacramental life of the Church, recognizing the abundant grace that flowed into her life through the sacraments, enriching her spiritual journey.

"Prayer is the breath of the soul, a constant conversation with God that sustains and uplifts us."

Application: Saint Scholastica's life was characterized by a deep life of prayer. She saw prayer as the breath of the soul, a constant conversation with God that sustained and uplifted her, guiding her in her spiritual journey and fostering intimacy with the Divine.

"Humility is not weakness, but strength in surrendering our own ego for the sake of God's glory."

Application: Saint Scholastica embodied humility in her life as a nun. She recognized that true humility was not weakness but strength in surrendering her own ego for the sake of God's glory, embracing a life of selflessness and service to others.

"Obedience is the path to true freedom, as we align our will with God's perfect plan for our lives."

Application: Saint Scholastica practiced obedience to God's will and the Rule of Saint Benedict. She understood that obedience was the path to true freedom, as she aligned her will with God's perfect plan for her life, finding fulfillment and purpose in her vocation as a nun.

"Penance is a humble response to our shortcomings, a way to grow closer to God and seek His forgiveness."

Application: Saint Scholastica embraced penance as a means of spiritual growth and reconciliation with God. She humbly acknowledged her shortcomings and sought forgiveness through acts of penance, recognizing it as a way to grow closer to God and deepen her relationship with Him.

"Charity is the fragrance of Christ, permeating our actions and drawing others closer to His love."

Application: Saint Scholastica's life was characterized by charity, which radiated the love of Christ to those around her. Her acts of charity permeated her actions, drawing others closer to Christ's love and inspiring them to follow His example of selfless love.

"Ora et labora, the sacred dance of prayer and work, where we find God's presence in every moment."

Application: Saint Scholastica embraced "ora et labora" (pray and work) as a sacred rhythm of monastic life. She saw prayer and work as a sacred dance where she found God's presence in every moment, allowing her to live fully immersed in His grace and love.

These applications demonstrate how the principles in these quotes were lived out in the life and teachings of Saint Scholastica, profoundly influencing her spirituality and the community she led.

31. "The Holy Eucharist is the ultimate expression of God's love, as He gives Himself completely for our nourishment and salvation."

32. "The sacraments are windows to heaven, where God pours out His grace and transforms our lives."

33. "Prayer is a sanctuary for the soul, a place where we encounter God's peace and find solace in His presence."

34. "Humility is the doorway to wisdom, as we recognize our own limitations and open ourselves to God's guidance."

35. "Obedience is a sign of trust, surrendering our own desires in order to align ourselves with God's perfect will."

36. "Penance is a path of healing, allowing us to confront our faults and seek reconciliation with God and others."

37. "Charity is a flame that burns brightly, warming the hearts of those in need and illuminating the path to God."

38. "Ora et labora, the rhythm of prayer and work, where we find balance and purpose in our daily lives."

39. "The Holy Eucharist is a sacred encounter with Christ, where we are united with Him in a profound and intimate way."

40. "The sacraments are tangible signs of God's grace, transforming ordinary moments into sacred encounters."

"The Holy Eucharist is the ultimate expression of God's love, as He gives Himself completely for our nourishment and salvation."

Application: Saint Benedict deeply revered the Holy Eucharist as the ultimate expression of God's love. He emphasized the importance of the Eucharist in the spiritual life of his monks, recognizing it as the source of nourishment and salvation for their souls.

"The sacraments are windows to heaven, where God pours out His grace and transforms our lives."

Application: Saint Benedict saw the sacraments as channels of God's grace that transformed the lives of his monks. He emphasized the importance of participating devoutly in the sacraments, recognizing them as windows to heaven where God poured out His grace abundantly.

"Prayer is a sanctuary for the soul, a place where we encounter God's peace and find solace in His presence."

Application: Saint Benedict valued prayer as a sanctuary for the soul. He structured the monastic day around the Liturgy of the Hours, creating a rhythm of prayer that allowed his monks to encounter God's peace and find solace in His presence amidst the busyness of daily life.

"Humility is the doorway to wisdom, as we recognize our own limitations and open ourselves to God's guidance."

Application: Saint Benedict emphasized humility as essential for spiritual growth and wisdom. He taught his monks to recognize their own limitations and to open themselves to God's guidance through humble submission to His will and the authority of the abbot.

"Obedience is a sign of trust, surrendering our own desires in order to align ourselves with God's perfect will."

Application: Saint Benedict placed a strong emphasis on obedience in his Rule. He saw obedience as a sign of trust in God's providence, teaching his monks to surrender their own desires in order to align themselves with God's perfect will as expressed through the Rule and the abbot.

"Penance is a path of healing, allowing us to confront our faults and seek reconciliation with God and others."

Application: Saint Benedict viewed penance as a path of healing for the soul. He encouraged his monks to confront their faults through acts of penance, seeking reconciliation with God and others as a means of spiritual growth and renewal.

"Charity is a flame that burns brightly, warming the hearts of those in need and illuminating the path to God."

Application: Saint Benedict exemplified charity through his hospitality and care for others. He saw charity as a flame that warmed the hearts of those in need, illuminating the path to God through acts of kindness and compassion.

"Ora et labora, the rhythm of prayer and work, where we find balance and purpose in our daily lives."

Application: Saint Benedict embraced the motto "ora et labora" (pray and work) as the foundation of monastic life. He saw prayer and work as a rhythm that provided balance and purpose in the daily lives of his monks, fostering spiritual and practical growth.

"The Holy Eucharist is a sacred encounter with Christ, where we are united with Him in a profound and intimate way."

Application: Saint Benedict taught his monks to approach the Holy Eucharist as a sacred encounter with Christ. He emphasized the profound and intimate union with Christ that occurred during the Eucharistic liturgy, nourishing their souls and deepening their relationship with God.

"The sacraments are tangible signs of God's grace, transforming ordinary moments into sacred encounters."

Application: Saint Benedict recognized the sacraments as tangible signs of God's grace. He taught his monks to approach the sacraments with reverence, recognizing their power to transform ordinary moments into sacred encounters with the divine, enriching their spiritual lives.

These applications demonstrate how the principles in these quotes were lived out in the life and teachings of Saint Benedict, profoundly influencing Saint Benedictine spirituality and monastic practices.

31. "The Holy Eucharist is the ultimate expression of God's love, as He gives Himself completely for our nourishment and salvation."

32. "The sacraments are windows to heaven, where God pours out His grace and transforms our lives."

33. "Prayer is a sanctuary for the soul, a place where we encounter God's peace and find solace in His presence."

34. "Humility is the doorway to wisdom, as we recognize our own limitations and open ourselves to God's guidance."

35. "Obedience is a sign of trust, surrendering our own desires in order to align ourselves with God's perfect will."

36. "Penance is a path of healing, allowing us to confront our faults and seek reconciliation with God and others."

37. "Charity is a flame that burns brightly, warming the hearts of those in need and illuminating the path to God."

38. "Ora et labora, the rhythm of prayer and work, where we find balance and purpose in our daily lives."

39. "The Holy Eucharist is a sacred encounter with Christ, where we are united with Him in a profound and intimate way."

40. "The sacraments are tangible signs of God's grace, transforming ordinary moments into sacred encounters."

"The Holy Eucharist is the ultimate expression of God's love, as He gives Himself completely for our nourishment and salvation."

Application: Saint Scholastica deeply revered the Holy Eucharist as the ultimate expression of God's love. She participated devoutly in the Eucharistic liturgy, recognizing it as a profound manifestation of God's self-giving love for humanity, nourishing her soul and deepening her faith.

"The sacraments are windows to heaven, where God pours out His grace and transforms our lives."

Application: Saint Scholastica understood the sacraments as channels of God's grace that transformed lives. She valued the sacraments as sacred encounters with the divine, where God poured out His grace abundantly, enriching her spiritual journey and fostering her growth in holiness.

"Prayer is a sanctuary for the soul, a place where we encounter God's peace and find solace in His presence."

Application: Saint Scholastica cherished prayer as a sanctuary for her soul. She spent dedicated time in prayer, seeking God's peace and finding solace in His presence amidst the challenges of life, nurturing a deep and intimate relationship with God.

"Humility is the doorway to wisdom, as we recognize our own limitations and open ourselves to God's guidance."

Application: Saint Scholastica exemplified humility in her life. She recognized her own limitations and weaknesses, opening herself to God's guidance and wisdom through humble submission to His will, cultivating a spirit of humility that led her closer to God.

"Obedience is a sign of trust, surrendering our own desires in order to align ourselves with God's perfect will."

Application: Saint Scholastica practiced obedience as a sign of trust in God's providence. She submitted herself to the Rule of Saint Benedict and the authority of her abbess, surrendering her own desires in order to align herself with God's perfect will, finding true freedom and fulfillment in obedience.

"Penance is a path of healing, allowing us to confront our faults and seek reconciliation with God and others."

Application: Saint Scholastica embraced penance as a path of healing for the soul. She humbly confronted her faults and shortcomings, seeking reconciliation with God and others through acts of penance, fostering spiritual growth and deepening her relationship with God.

"Charity is a flame that burns brightly, warming the hearts of those in need and illuminating the path to God."

Application: Saint Scholastica lived a life of charity, showing kindness and compassion to others. She saw charity as a flame that warmed the hearts of those in need, illuminating the path to God through her selfless acts of love and service to others.

"Ora et labora, the rhythm of prayer and work, where we find balance and purpose in our daily lives."

Application: Saint Scholastica embraced the Saint Benedictine motto "ora et labora" (pray and work) in her life as a nun. She found balance and purpose in her daily life through the rhythm of prayer and work, recognizing them as essential components of her vocation and spiritual growth.

"The Holy Eucharist is a sacred encounter with Christ, where we are united with Him in a profound and intimate way."

Application: Saint Scholastica approached the Holy Eucharist as a sacred encounter with Christ. She recognized the profound and intimate union with Christ that occurred during the Eucharistic liturgy, where she was united with Him in a deeply spiritual and transformative way.

"The sacraments are tangible signs of God's grace, transforming ordinary moments into sacred encounters."

Application: Saint Scholastica valued the sacraments as tangible signs of God's grace. She saw them as transformative encounters with the divine, transforming ordinary moments into sacred encounters where she experienced God's presence and grace in a tangible way.

These applications demonstrate how the principles in these quotes were lived out in the life and teachings of Saint Scholastica, profoundly influencing her spirituality and her role as a leader in the Saint Benedictine tradition.

41. "Prayer is the conversation of the soul with its Creator, a bridge that connects us to the divine."

42. "Humility is the recognition that all we have comes from God, and it is through His grace that we are able to accomplish anything."

43. "Obedience is the path of trust and surrender, allowing God to lead and guide us in His perfect wisdom."

44. "Penance is a humble response to our own brokenness, a way to seek reconciliation and grow closer to God's mercy."

45. "Charity is the embodiment of God's love in action, a selfless giving of oneself for the well-being of others."

46. "Ora et labora, the integration of prayer and work, where we find fulfillment and purpose in our daily tasks."

47. "The Holy Eucharist is a sacred banquet, where we partake in the body and blood of Christ, nourishing our souls and strengthening our faith."

48. "The sacraments are channels of God's grace, transforming ordinary moments into sacred encounters with the divine."

49. "Prayer is the anchor that keeps us grounded in the midst of life's challenges, reminding us of God's presence and faithfulness."

50. "Humility is the virtue that opens the door to God's grace, allowing Him to work in and through us for His glory."

"Prayer is the conversation of the soul with its Creator, a bridge that connects us to the divine."

Application: Saint Benedict prioritized prayer as the cornerstone of his spiritual life. He saw prayer as a conversation with God, a bridge that connected him to the divine, fostering intimacy with his Creator and guiding him in all aspects of his life.

"Humility is the recognition that all we have comes from God, and it is through His grace that we are able to accomplish anything."

Application: Saint Benedict embodied humility in his life, recognizing that all his gifts and accomplishments were due to God's grace. He humbly attributed everything to God, acknowledging his dependence on divine assistance in all his endeavors.

"Obedience is the path of trust and surrender, allowing God to lead and guide us in His perfect wisdom."

Application: Saint Benedict placed a strong emphasis on obedience in his Rule. He viewed obedience as a path of trust and surrender to God's will, allowing God to lead and guide him and his monks in His perfect wisdom through the authority of the abbot.

"Penance is a humble response to our own brokenness, a way to seek reconciliation and grow closer to God's mercy."

Application: Saint Benedict understood the importance of penance in the spiritual life. He taught his monks to engage in acts of penance as a humble response to their own brokenness, seeking reconciliation with God and growing closer to His mercy through sincere repentance.

"Charity is the embodiment of God's love in action, a selfless giving of oneself for the well-being of others."

Application: Saint Benedict exemplified charity in his life through his hospitality and care for others. He saw charity as the embodiment of God's love in action, teaching his monks to practice selfless giving for the well-being of others, particularly through the Saint Benedictine principle of hospitality.

"Ora et labora, the integration of prayer and work, where we find fulfillment and purpose in our daily tasks."

Application: Saint Benedict embraced the motto "ora et labora" (pray and work) as the foundation of monastic life. He integrated prayer and work seamlessly, recognizing them as complementary activities that brought fulfillment and purpose to daily tasks in the monastery.

"The Holy Eucharist is a sacred banquet, where we partake in the body and blood of Christ, nourishing our souls and strengthening our faith."

Application: Saint Benedict held the Holy Eucharist in deep reverence. He saw the Eucharist as a sacred banquet where he and his monks partook in the body and blood of Christ, nourishing their souls and strengthening their faith in the mystery of Christ's presence.

"The sacraments are channels of God's grace, transforming ordinary moments into sacred encounters with the divine."

Application: Saint Benedict recognized the sacraments as channels of God's grace. He taught his monks to approach the sacraments with reverence, seeing them as transformative encounters with the divine that elevated ordinary moments into sacred encounters with God's presence and grace.

"Prayer is the anchor that keeps us grounded in the midst of life's challenges, reminding us of God's presence and faithfulness."

Application: Saint Benedict relied on prayer as an anchor in the midst of life's challenges. He understood prayer as a source of strength and stability, reminding him and his monks of God's constant presence and faithfulness, even in the face of difficulties.

"Humility is the virtue that opens the door to God's grace, allowing Him to work in and through us for His glory."

Application: Saint Benedict valued humility as a virtue that opened the door to God's grace. He believed that humility allowed God to work in and through him and his monks for His glory, recognizing that true greatness came from humble service and obedience to God's will.

These applications demonstrate how the principles in these quotes were lived out in the life and teachings of Saint Benedict, profoundly influencing Saint Benedictine spirituality and the monastic tradition.

41. "Prayer is the conversation of the soul with its Creator, a bridge that connects us to the divine."

42. "Humility is the recognition that all we have comes from God, and it is through His grace that we are able to accomplish anything."

43. "Obedience is the path of trust and surrender, allowing God to lead and guide us in His perfect wisdom."

44. "Penance is a humble response to our own brokenness, a way to seek reconciliation and grow closer to God's mercy."

45. "Charity is the embodiment of God's love in action, a selfless giving of oneself for the well-being of others."

46. "Ora et labora, the integration of prayer and work, where we find fulfillment and purpose in our daily tasks."

47. "The Holy Eucharist is a sacred banquet, where we partake in the body and blood of Christ, nourishing our souls and strengthening our faith."

48. "The sacraments are channels of God's grace, transforming ordinary moments into sacred encounters with the divine."

49. "Prayer is the anchor that keeps us grounded in the midst of life's challenges, reminding us of God's presence and faithfulness."

50. "Humility is the virtue that opens the door to God's grace, allowing Him to work in and through us for His glory."

"Prayer is the conversation of the soul with its Creator, a bridge that connects us to the divine."

Application: Saint Scholastica devoted herself to prayer, considering it as a profound conversation with God. Through prayer, she sought to deepen her relationship with her Creator, viewing it as a bridge that connected her soul to the divine, fostering intimacy and communion with God.

"Humility is the recognition that all we have comes from God, and it is through His grace that we are able to accomplish anything."

Application: Saint Scholastica embodied humility in her life, acknowledging that all her gifts and accomplishments were due to God's grace. She recognized her own dependence on God, attributing everything to His providence and grace, which empowered her to accomplish great things for His glory.

"Obedience is the path of trust and surrender, allowing God to lead and guide us in His perfect wisdom."

Application: Saint Scholastica embraced obedience as a path of trust and surrender to God's will. She submitted herself to the authority of her abbess and the Rule of Saint Benedict, trusting that God would lead and guide her in His perfect wisdom through obedience to His divine will.

"Penance is a humble response to our own brokenness, a way to seek reconciliation and grow closer to God's mercy."

Application: Saint Scholastica practiced penance as a humble response to her own brokenness. She engaged in acts of penance to seek reconciliation with God and grow closer to His mercy, recognizing the need for repentance and spiritual growth in her journey towards holiness.

"Charity is the embodiment of God's love in action, a selfless giving of oneself for the well-being of others."

Application: Saint Scholastica lived a life of charity, demonstrating God's love in action through selfless giving for the well-being of others. She showed kindness and compassion to those in need, embodying the selfless love of Christ in her interactions and service to others.

"Ora et labora, the integration of prayer and work, where we find fulfillment and purpose in our daily tasks."

Application: Saint Scholastica embraced the Saint Benedictine motto "ora et labora" (pray and work) in her life as a nun. She integrated prayer and work seamlessly, finding fulfillment and purpose in her daily tasks through the rhythm of prayer and work, recognizing them as integral components of her vocation and spiritual growth.

"The Holy Eucharist is a sacred banquet, where we partake in the body and blood of Christ, nourishing our souls and strengthening our faith."

Application: Saint Scholastica held the Holy Eucharist in deep reverence. She viewed the Eucharist as a sacred banquet where she partook in the body and blood of Christ, nourishing her soul and strengthening her faith in the mystery of Christ's presence and love.

"The sacraments are channels of God's grace, transforming ordinary moments into sacred encounters with the divine."

Application: Saint Scholastica recognized the sacraments as channels of God's grace. She approached the sacraments with reverence, seeing them as transformative encounters with the divine that elevated ordinary moments into sacred encounters with God's presence and grace.

"Prayer is the anchor that keeps us grounded in the midst of life's challenges, reminding us of God's presence and faithfulness."

Application: Saint Scholastica relied on prayer as an anchor in the midst of life's challenges. She understood prayer as a source of strength and stability, reminding her of God's presence and faithfulness even in difficult times, anchoring her soul in the midst of life's storms.

"Humility is the virtue that opens the door to God's grace, allowing Him to work in and through us for His glory."

Application: Saint Scholastica valued humility as a virtue that opened the door to God's grace. She believed that humility allowed God to work in and through her for His glory, recognizing that true greatness came from humble service and obedience to God's will.

These applications demonstrate how the principles in these quotes were lived out in the life and teachings of Saint Scholastica, profoundly influencing her spirituality and her role as a leader in the Saint Benedictine tradition.